ULTIMA THULE

Simone Sassen

ULTIMA THULE

A Journey to Spitsbergen

Photographs with an essay

by Cees Nooteboom

Schirmer/Mosel

In September 2007, Cees Nooteboom and several other writer-travelers accepted an invitation from the Norwegian Ministry of Foreign Affairs to visit the extreme north of the country, namely Tromsø, Spitsbergen, Hammerfest, and Kirkenes. The occasion was the International Polar Year 2007/2008. The aim of the tour was to draw attention to the far-reaching developments in this both climatically and politically sensitive region. Only recently has new Russian activity here made it clear that the nation has a stalwart interest in the area, although cooperation between the countries concerned, namely Russia, Finland, Norway, and Sweden, continues to be relaxed in this region.

The writers invited were Redmond O'Hanlon, Great Britain; Alberto Manguel, Canada; Cees Nooteboom, the Netherlands; Lieve Joris, Belgium; Marc de Gouvain, France; Thomas Boberg, Denmark; Tété-Michel Kpomassie, Congo; and Kjartan Fløgstad, Norway.

The project entitled "Ultima Thule" – the proverbial land at the northern edge of the world – was accompanied by a Norwegian television crew, the video artist Patricia Davelouis (Peru), the photographer Bjarne Riesto, and as a guest Simone Sassen.

I

Towards the North by Plane

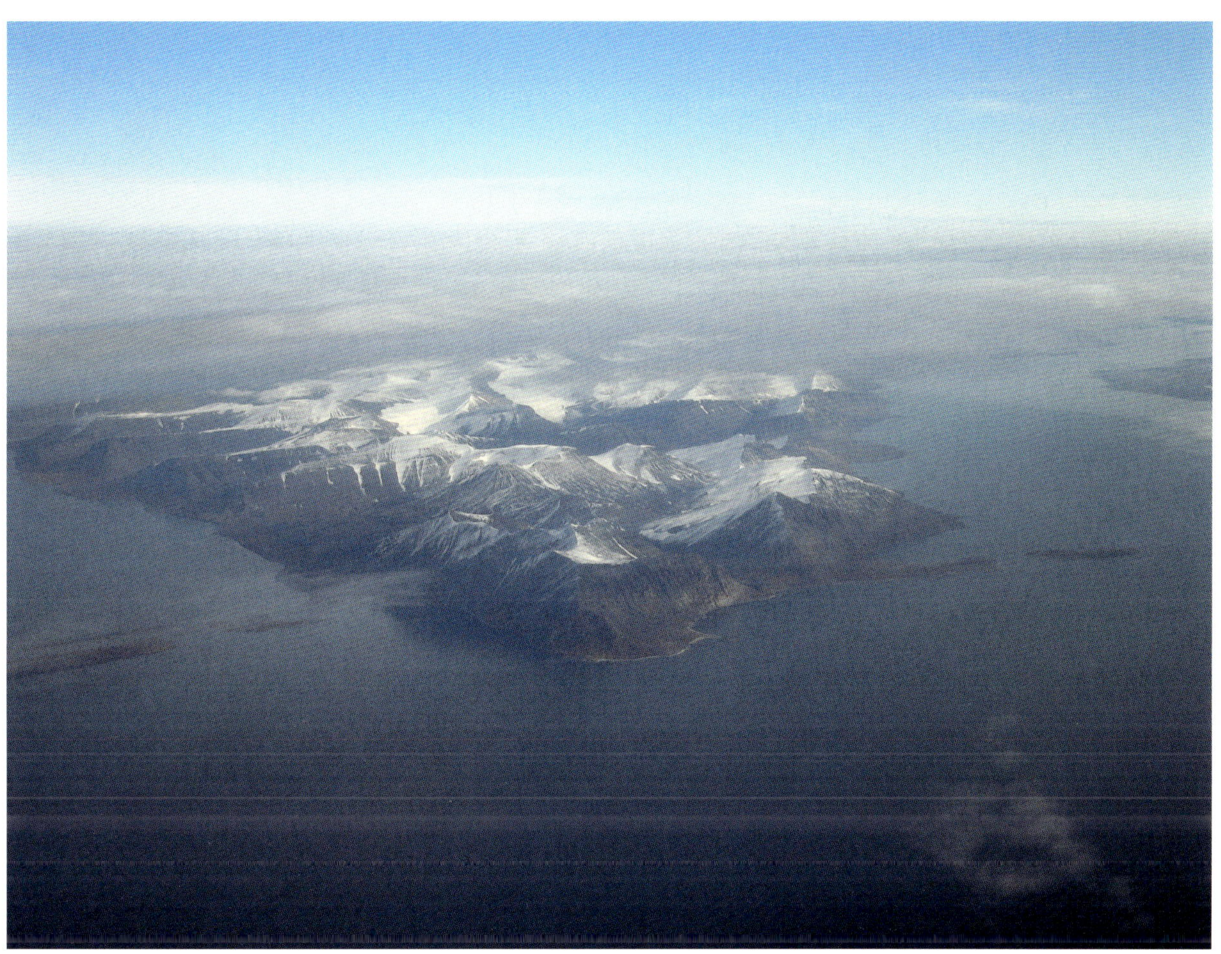

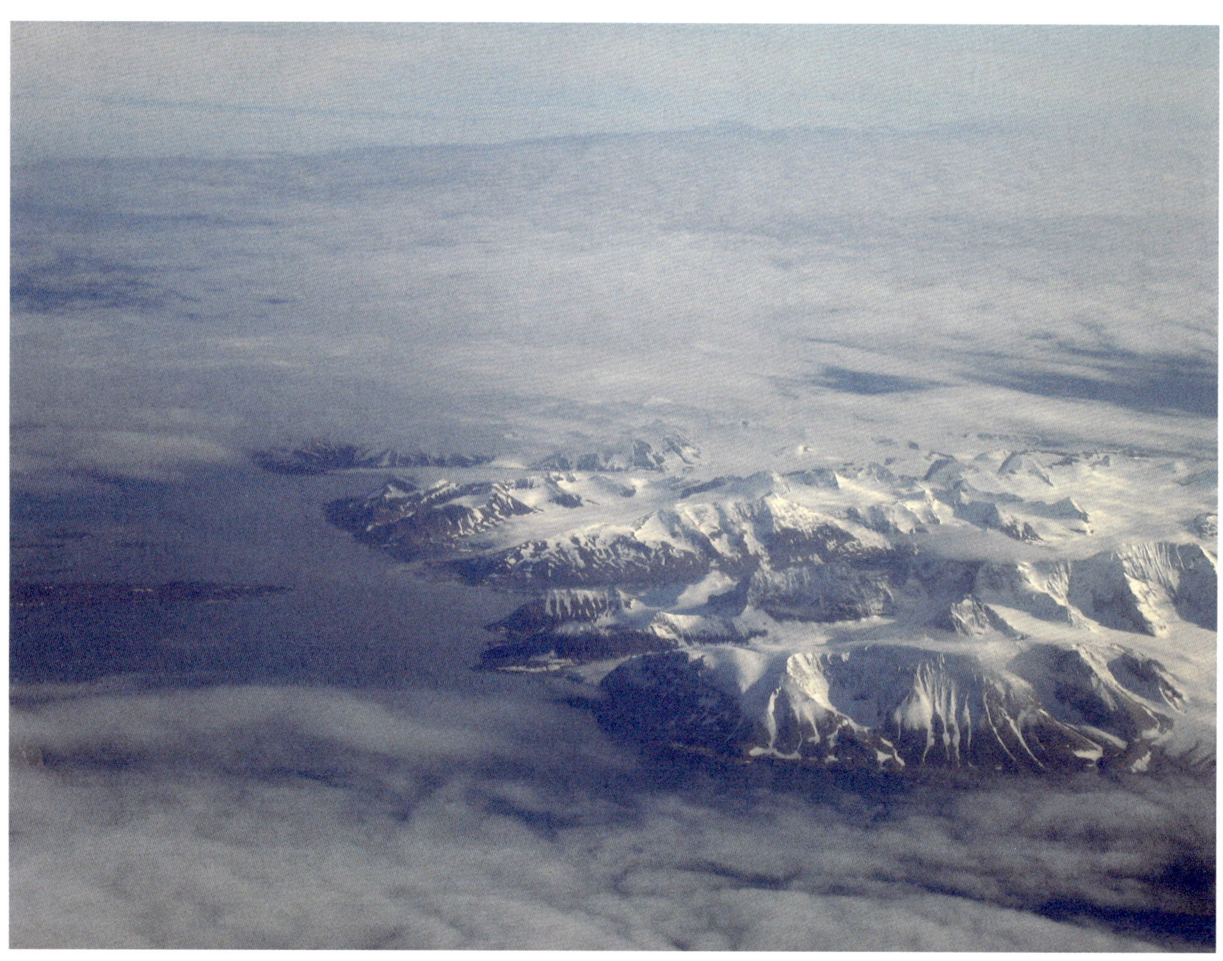

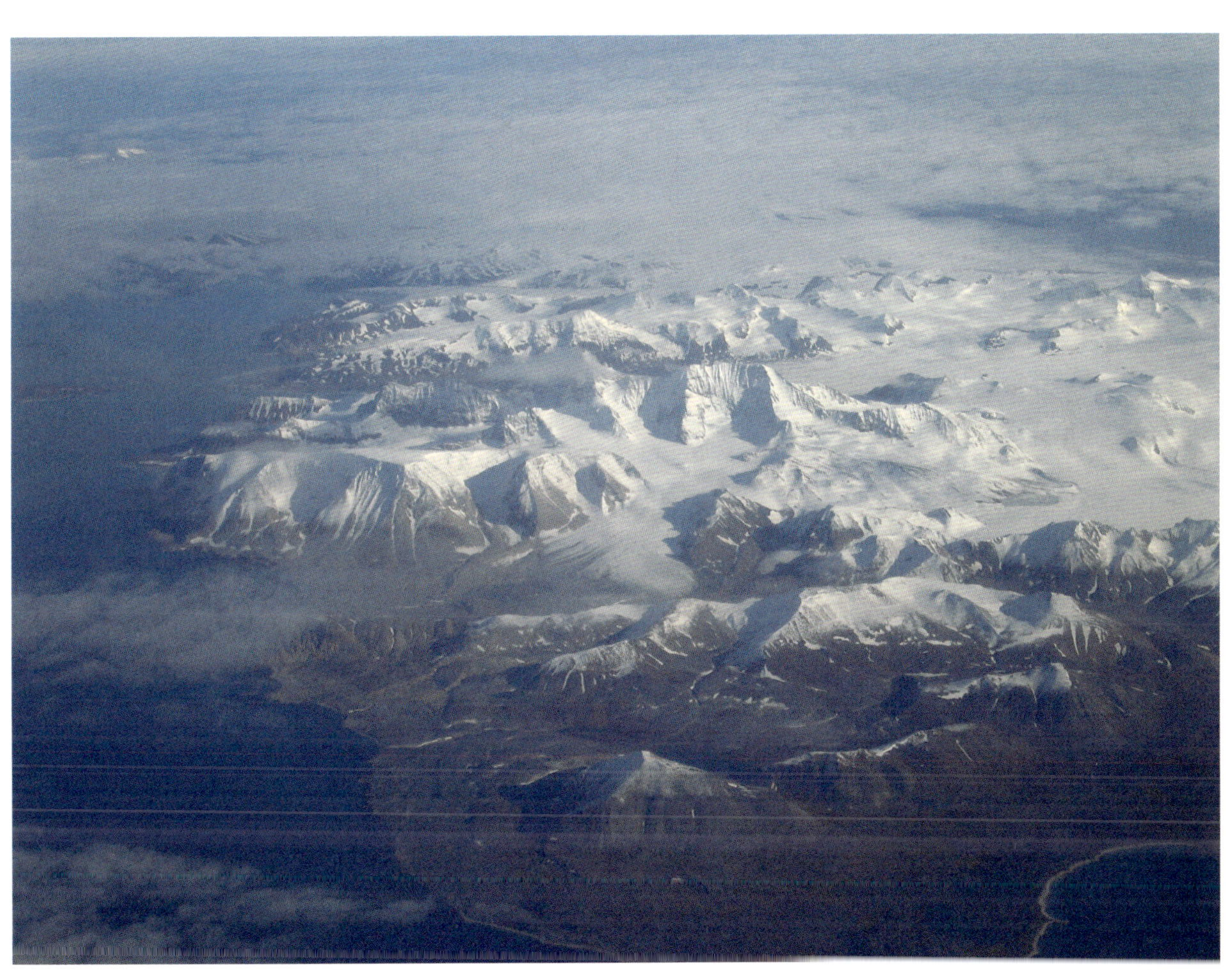

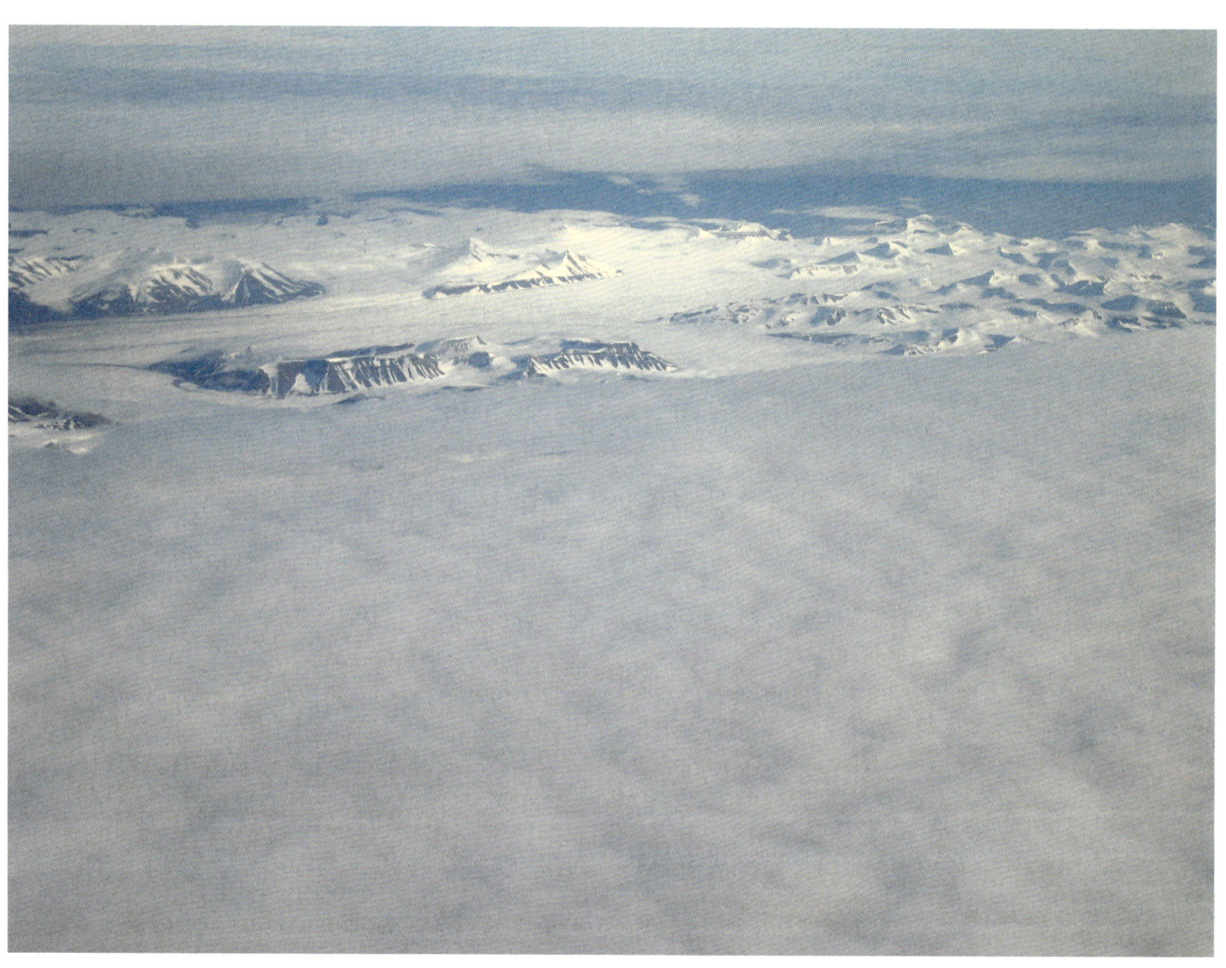

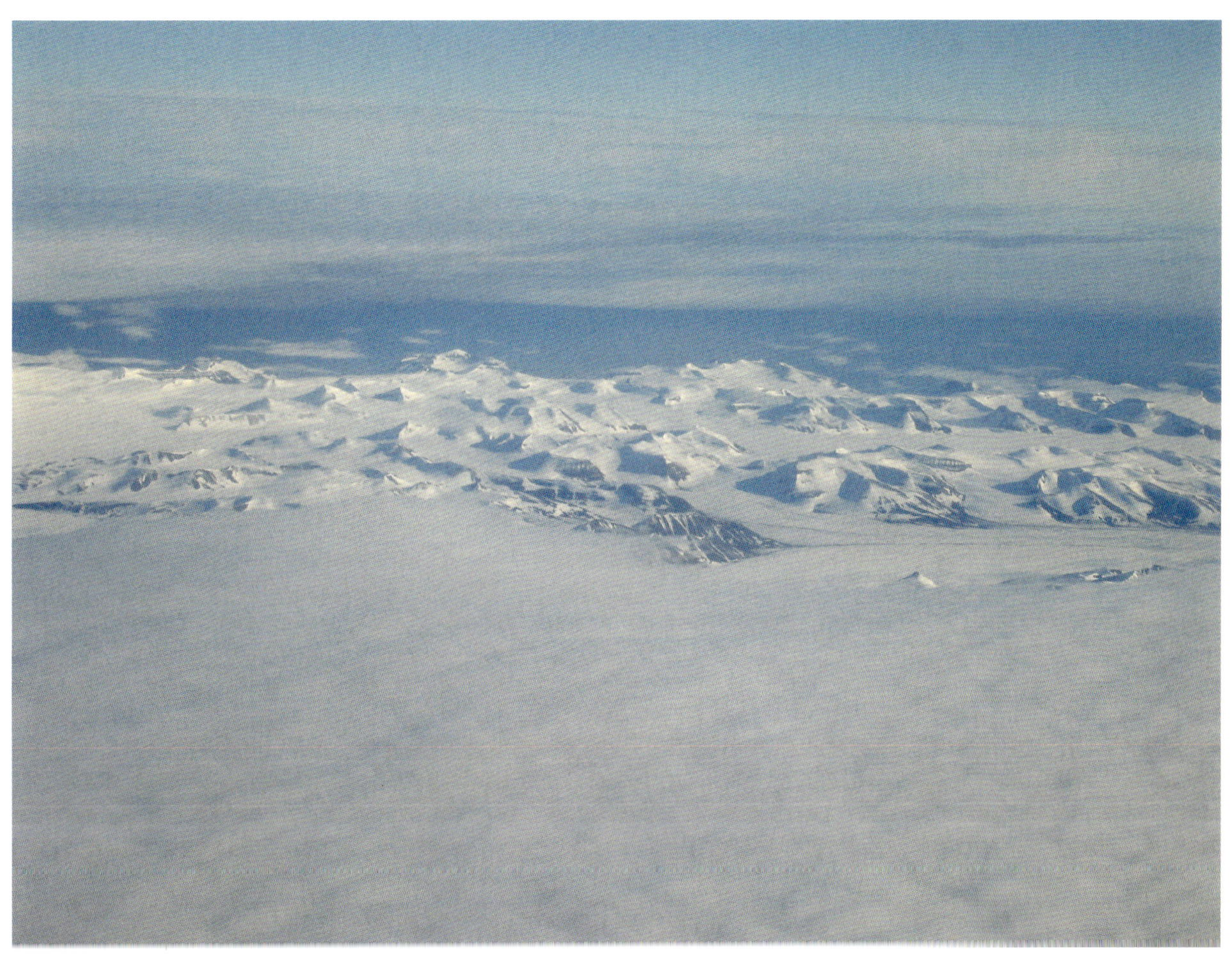

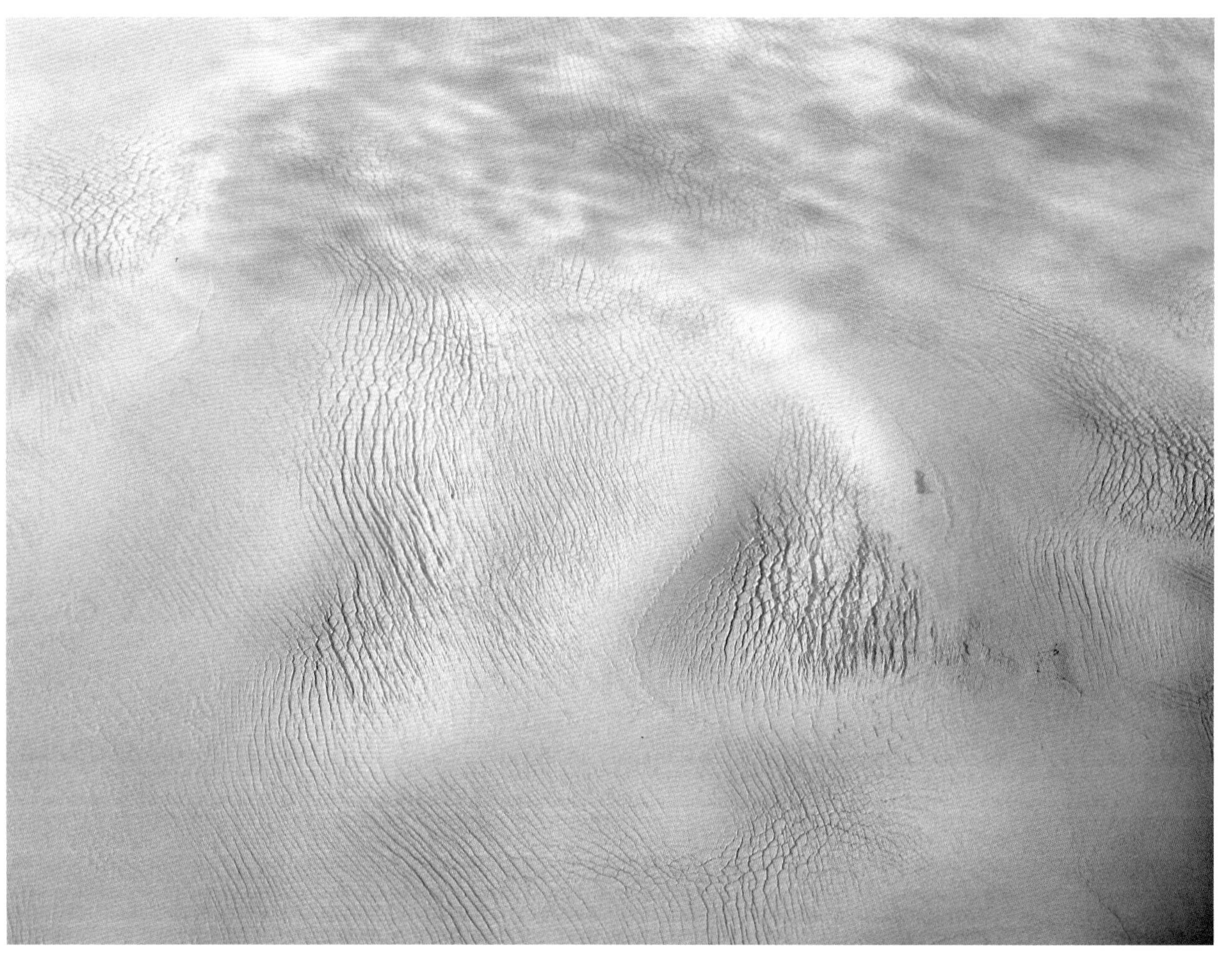

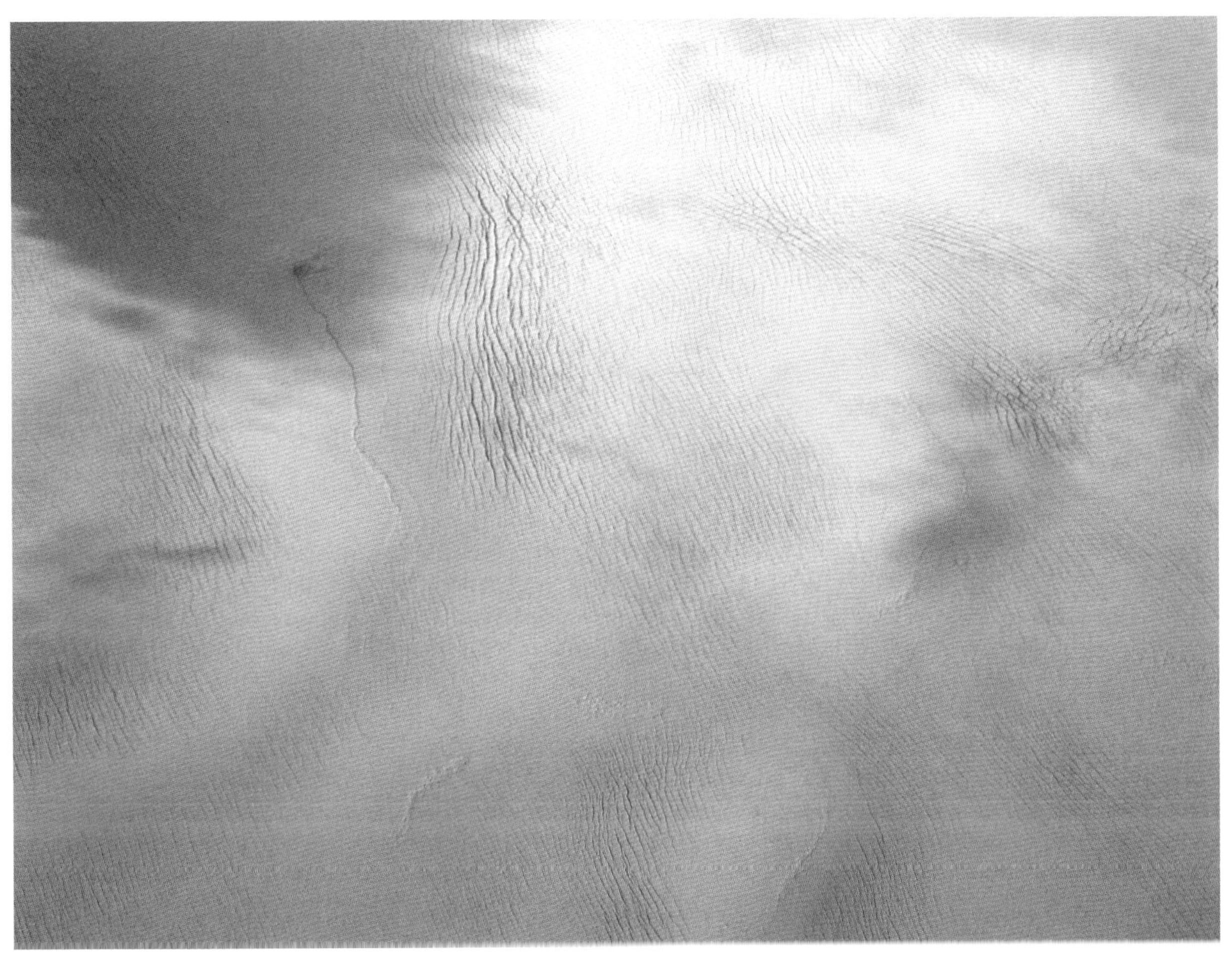

II

Ultima Thule. A Journey to Spitsbergen

CEES NOOTEBOOM

1. On the flight from Oslo to Tromsø, two worlds: the land far below me, the map on my lap. Outside, the sun is setting. The clouds hanging over the land on my map have been painted by Max Ernst, surreal, puffy sky formations, squadrons whizzing past us, fire within the grey, the land below already dark, less and less visible, a mere assumption. And mysterious as it may be, it can't be chaos because roads have been drawn on the map, there are towns, harbours, names. The thin green lines are provincial borders; the thicker ones indicate where in that immensity one country begins, the other ends – Russia, Finland, Norway. We, a small group of travellers who write, have been invited by the Norwegian government to spend a week in the Arctic regions. Our hosts have called our expedition "Ultima Thule," a metaphorical title used by Nabokov, who probably drew his inspiration for his story – which had little to do with the real Spitsbergen – from the same antique associations that stir anyone who hears the name for the first time: *Ultima*, the very last, the very farthest land at the end of the world, just before true infinity begins. The nostalgia the phrase conveys is shared by all travellers. The name turns up very early in an account by Greek geographer and navigator Pytheas of Massilia, who was never there himself and, on the famous ancient Carta Marina of Olaus Magnus, the land lies small, round and alienated from its real shape directly above an equally imagined and drawn whale among wildly striped waves. Whether our trip has something to do with the recent unrest surrounding the Pole and the sudden Russian territorial claims, I don't know. Anyhow, nobody mentions anything about it. In the far-off northern towns on our itinerary,

we will be visiting libraries and museums, as well as a university, the headquarters of the oil industry and a fish processing plant – rather like the Queen on a working visit.

Our first destination, Spitsbergen, lies so far to the Arctic north that it's off the map, while the map itself is so large and detailed I am having trouble locating those places that next week will suddenly change from names into reality – Tromsø, Hammerfest, Kirkenes, places far apart from one another in an infinity of land, bays, fjords, islands, lakes. Those who are impervious to the lure of maps and the craving they cause will find it difficult to imagine my excitement: thousands of square kilometres without any roads, beige and pale green expanses with, again and again, the blue of the sea or an inland waterway; names in Finnish or Norwegian identifying mountains and plains, or rivers whose banks are devoid of villages or towns – existing geographical places that I'll never visit, the lure of the impossible. Gabmaskaide, Doaresjokrassa, Kipperfjordfjellet, a cantilena of the truly inaccessible and yet real, mapped, measured, drawn.

In the newspaper that I am unable to read, the weather report shows water colours of clouds with a sun behind them. Later in the week, daytime temperatures will range from two to five degrees Celsius in Tromsø, from one to four degrees in Longyearbyen, the capital of Spitsbergen. We are beginning our descent. All that is left from the sun is some silverware, but then that is gone, too. The lower layer of clouds has fattened, it stretches to the horizon like an enormous slab of mouldy lard until we break through it in the midst of rainy squalls. And suddenly all those islands on the map are for real, I can see Tromsø's lights and hills. An hour later I am walking along rain-drenched streets, past the Domkirke, painted yellowish brown, past a café with Russian girls, past the steep rise of the Arctic Cathedral. The picture I saw in photographs – vividly coloured wooden houses next to steel blue water – is wiped away: all of a sudden I am in a low, northern provincial town that smells of sea and distance. From here, we will leave tomorrow morning for Svalbard, as the Norwegians prefer to call the archipelago. Svalbard: Cold Coast. Before we move on, I drop by a low wooden house painted red on the waterfront, the Polarmuseet, a grim reality reduced to *tableaux vivants* which, awkward though they may be, nevertheless convey something of the extreme conditions: a rigid, solitary fisherman rowing between ice floes; the monumental skeleton of a walrus, his unimaginable penis next to him; in front of the house the huge head of Amundsen with a nose like an icebreaker, swathed in Dante's headdress; sitting against the wooden beams of a fake cabin the dummy of a sailor plucking a snow goose, his rifle and the unpainted wooden slats that are his skis standing beside him. Brother Bear, terrifyingly large, Sister Fox, pointed and wily, deceptive, almost alive, animals mounted like religious relics, the melancholy head of a seal, photographs of glaciers and snowed-in cabins, whalers and blizzards – everything speaks of danger and desolation, humans and animals in combat with the elements and each other. Death plays the leading part. I have read enough stories about polar expeditions to fill in the rest. Arctic foxes, hung on the wall; then under glass I see their delicate skull so surprisingly small with vicious teeth. In another display case the nasty trap with which a polar bear can shoot itself. I know how close I am to that world, and yet I am not.

The next night, at the hotel in Longyearbyen, it will get even worse. You sit at a table with a glass of wine and you know you are barely more than a thousand kilometres from the Pole. For a few thousand dollars you can go there in an old Russian helicopter, and for one frivolous moment you will no longer be able to reconcile all those earlier stories with the luxury and safety that surround you. Willem Barents, the hibernation on Novaya Zemlya, Amundsen, Nansen, Scott, the stories about scurvy and death from starvation, the solitary graves all over this archipelago. In his book *The Terrors of Ice and Darkness*, Christoph Ransmayr gives a horrifying description of the epic expedition of Julius Payer and Carl Weyprecht, who in 1874 were trapped in the ice with their ship, the *Admiral Tegetthoff*, and had to haul their lifeboats on foot over the brutal ice field until they finally reached open water and were rescued by a Russian whaler. The only faint reminder of this is that you are asked not to go into the hills around the town alone and definitely not unarmed, because the bears that live here are often hungry and, if they have to, they'll make a meal of a human. If you carry no weapons yourself, you need to take someone along.

II. My first glimpse of Spitsbergen is from the air, and I see what the Dutchman Barents saw: pointed mountain peaks, *spitse bergen*. In the book *No Man's Land*, by Sir Martin Conway (Cambridge, 1906; facsimile published in Oslo, 1995), I read about those earliest days. On May 18, 1596, two ships set off from Vlieland, the Netherlands, with Willem Barents and Jacob van Heemskerck on one, and Jan Cornelisz Rijp on the other. On June 9, they stopped at what is called Bear Island in the book. Eight men from each ship went ashore with two open boats. They found a large quantity of gulls' eggs on the shore, but after going up a great hill of snow, they nearly broke their necks during the descent because of the steep slope with many dangerous rocks at the foot of it, so they decided to slide down on their backsides. Three days later they saw a "white bear," which they wanted to catch, but the animal was so large they didn't dare. They rowed back to the ship and got muskets, halberts and axes. For four bells (two hours) they fought with the bear, which swam away with an axe in its back, but eventually they caught it. They ate some of the flesh, but it disagreed with them, and they were lucky that was all it did, since a lot of Arctic explorers have died from eating polar-bear meat; the liver in particular can be toxic. They named the island Beeren Eylandt (now Bjørnøya) and continued northward on June 13. The following morning – they were probably far off shore yet, at 78°15′ – they saw land west of what they named the Grooten Inwyck and is now called the Isfjorden.

On the sixteenth they encountered pack ice and proceeded east. At 80°10′ they sighted "high land, entirely covered with snow," the north coast of Spitsbergen. They sailed back and forth for a week, and dropped anchor. The land, they later said, was "broken and consisted only of mountains and pointed hills, for which reason we gave it the name of 'Spitsbergen.'" Because they thought they were in Greenland, they didn't know they had discovered an island. Yet, fortunately, they happily kept on assigning names. If, for example, they couldn't get through because of the ice, they turned around and named that inland waterway Keerwyck ("Turn Around Inlet"), or if they found the huge teeth of a walrus, they called that spot Tandenbaai ("Teeth Bay") and, while they were at it, took formal possession of the land by leaving behind a record of their visit. The rest is history. Rijp and Barents went their separate ways. Barents became icebound at Novaya Zemlya, wintered in the gloom of the barren, sunless icefield, built a house from driftwood and tried in the spring to reach the open sea – as the crew of the *Admiral Tegetthoff* would attempt many years later – but died of scurvy on the way on June 20. After a gruelling journey through the wilderness of ice, the others finally reached open water, where they discovered two Russian ships. Shortly thereafter they found scurvy-grass, which partially cured them, and then sailed straight across the sea to the mouth of the Petchora River, where they arrived on August 4. One month later, at Kola in the White Sea, by an incredible accident they encountered the ship of Jan Cornelisz Rijp, from whom they had parted over a year ago. Nearly three hundred years later Captain Elling Carlsen of Hammerfest found the ruins of Barents's hut, 16 metres long by 10 metres wide. He collected all kinds of objects that had been buried for all those centuries under a protective accumulation of ice. Along with 112 more relics from another expedition, they are now kept at the Rijksmuseum in Amsterdam.

It is evening in Longyearbyen. I have wandered through the narrow town. "Town" is perhaps too big a word, "settlement" would be better. Here, too, is a polar museum – bold, modern architecture. Everything I have just read becomes even more dramatic because of the pictures and the objects. Now I want to walk along the water for a bit. I have left the museum behind, and my layman's mind has a lot to mull over. At this late hour, the road is deserted and bleak. In the distance looms some kind of development. The water to my left is an inland waterway, the land around it the colour of rust. The distant hills are grey, rocky, capped with snow. This archipelago, of which Spitsbergen is the main island, is almost as large as the Netherlands and Belgium put together, yet the total population of all the settlements is less than 2,700. I am trying to take in what I just read: in the Mesozoic, 250 million years ago, Svalbard was situated where Spain is today – it has moved north on top of drifting tectonic plates – but if that already strikes me as odd, there are even more numbers and distances to confuse me because in still earlier days the archipelago, now 60 per cent ice, lay below the equator.

Time and again, the world has been boiled, it seems, and it sometimes boiled over. Mountain ridges have melted, cliff faces folded in half, stone types have been mixed together, and liquid magma has flowed to the surface and hardened into granite – a long, furious fairy tale in which rock was stretched into endless ribbons, swamps with all their vegetation turned into coal beds and dinosaurs appeared and vanished, while at the bottom of the cooking pot, below the later ice, fossils were preserved that tell about an earlier life when nature still managed without us.

Fog is setting in. My road, *vei 400*, leads to Adventdalen, but I won't go that far. In the dusk I see a distant light and decide to walk as far as that. When I come closer, I see it's a fenced-off piece of land filled with wooden kennels for huskies, waiting for winter. They are chained up, lying with their heads stuck out of the kennels' glassless windows. They aren't curious about me, they look right through me with those eerie, luminous eyes. I am nobody because I'm not coming to get them for a trip to the North Pole. Everything people say about animals is always interpretation: even when I say I think they are beautiful, it's probably nonsense. Yet there is an indescribable melancholy hanging over that place, and rejection, too, as though you ought to belong to another order to catch their attention, as though you should fit in better with the landscape. I am a passerby who has never been tested by danger, I have been tried and found wanting.

The following morning I have that feeling once again when I head the other way along the Sjoomradet towards the industrial complexes and the small port at the Adventfjorden, from where we'll set off by boat the next day for Pyramiden, an abandoned Russian mine. The utility buildings stand out vividly against the strong setting: cheerful colours, straight lines, the ships at the yard utterly still in the metallic water, hardly any people, and all this against a background of truncated, decapitated mountains on the opposite side, ponderous animals with snow-covered flanks. Gas tanks, factories, cars ... I don't know if it's because of the silence, but each building seems to be painted separately: pictures by a hyperrealist painter, who has added silence as an extra dimension. A ship the colour of dark red lead, an oil pipe, a tall factory tower with a single light – if a car happens to drive by, it's an event.

I wonder what it must be like when winter comes and the sun disappears for four months. Longyearbyen is the only town of some size; it has 1,800 inhabitants. To the southwest is the Russian coal mine Barentsburg, watched with a certain suspicion since the most recent Russian exercises around the Pole, with the Russians announcing that their landmass extends much further underneath the ice than had been assumed in the past, which could have major implications for the recovery of oil. As a result of a treaty concluded in the 1920s, Barentsburg is partially outside Norwegian jurisdiction. About 800 Russians still live there. Further north lies Ny Ålesund, with 40 souls. Anything north of that is inaccessible and usually off-limits. No roads link the settlements to Spitsbergen. There is also an automated weather station somewhere but, anyway, no one else lives here. Only during the brief summer, yachts sail along the inhospitable coasts of Nordaustlandet and Kvitøya. In January and February, temperatures in Longyearbyen can drop to below minus 40 degrees Celsius, and in March it's even colder – how do you live then? It's not so bad, is the reply, which is then followed rather provocatively by "and when winter's gone, we all change partners." It is a long night, the polar night, and I can already tell that those who haven't experienced it have no right to speak. What would it be like to come here in the winter? Still a bright sunrise at noon in November, followed instantly by twilight, but then a gradually deepening darkness. Walking in the dark to the modern library by the light of the stars or the moon (if it's out) just above the horizon and finally read everything there you have always meant to? How long can you keep going when you don't actually need to be here? What does one do all that time? You get used to it, they say, there are books, DVDs and CDs after all, people take adult-education courses at the university, there are all kinds of clubs, and then we have our work, of course. We really aren't dying of boredom, and unless there's a problem the Tromsø plane with the newspapers comes every day. And sometimes we have the northern lights …

III. The next morning we are crammed into a bus. Everybody looks dressed up. The boat trip to Pyramiden will take ten hours. We have been warned about the icy cold on the open water; thermal underwear has been recommended, so are hats, sunglasses because of the glaring light near the glaciers, sturdy shoes as some of the terrain where we'll go ashore is heavy going. I had no idea what to expect, yet I could tell from the rifles I saw standing somewhere that the excursion wasn't going to be altogether routine. Pyramiden, if I understood correctly, was an old Russian mine. Under the terms of international treaties dating back to the early twentieth century, including the one concerning Barentsburg, the Soviet Union had the right to exploit Pyramiden, as well as the mine at Barentsburg, still in operation. The exploitation continued even after the collapse of the Soviet Union, until suddenly one day in 1998 the entire population of Pyramiden picked up and left, abandoning the enormous complex to the Arctic winter. The Second World War had convinced both Germans and Russians of the strategic importance of coal for their navies in this part of the world, and the new Russian claims in the region show a persistent military and economic interest. There may also be oil, or gas, or goodness knows what under all that ice after all, and not surprisingly there are discussions going on about the exact location of maritime boundaries, but no one, except the Norwegians of course, is allowed to fish within 370 kilometres of the whole coastline. So, no matter what, it is in Norwegian waters that we put out to sea on the MS *Langøysund*.

Apart from the cold, I mainly remember the colour grey, and the immense forlornness of the landscape. Not a trace of a human presence anywhere. A Russian ship at anchor in the middle of a bay, a small wooden shack on a deserted stone beach – that is all we see for hours on end. Forlorn landscapes, is there such a thing? Probably not, but how can you feel any other way about those grey masses of rock standing with drab, weather-beaten spurs in the equally ashen water? The ship follows the coast, one vast accumulation of forbidding rock and stone without visible vegetation, land where by the look of it no human has ever set foot; bare, and yet sometimes rust-coloured or ochrous brown with moss; then, later, the dangerous glare from the Nordenskjold Glacier. The ship will try to get as close to it as possible, until we lie still in water like polished onyx full of small gleaming blocks of ice. The biologists among us are getting excited about the birds they spot: kittiwakes, ivory gulls, little auks, snow buntings and puffins. We are allowed the odd peek through their binoculars, but the birds are faster than our frozen movements; they live here. Around noon we enter Billefjorden, a branch of the broader Isfjorden. We spot Pyramiden portside, make a wide turn and tie up at a long landing place and some kind of tall, iron railway bridge over which trains used to run. Just before the Russians left, they tried to blow up the buildings along the quay, which was prevented by the Sysselman, the Norwegian governor of Svalbard. The mountains here are the colour of old leather, and the mountain that towers three thousand metres above everything is actually pyramid-shaped. Suddenly a few men we had assumed to be passengers have rifles slung over their backs in case we encounter a polar bear. In small, separate groups we walk across the boggy ground; when I look back I see a low cloud sailing along the landing place where the ship now lies deserted. We are only stopping here for a little over an hour, and it will be an hour in the dead past, in a communist Pompeii without corpses.

No volcano erupted here, but the effect is the same: it all looks as if suddenly one day the plague broke out. Buildings, the recreation centre, the large open square with the statue of Lenin, the swimming pool – everything is empty. Almost the first thing I see is a small wooden structure with a sign in Cyrillic lettering and below it, on the ground, the portraits of Marx and Lenin. Nobody took them along. In spite of everything, I can't help feeling somewhat fearful as I wander through the rooms – family photographs, work schedules, tipped-over table lamps – no wonder it all reminds me of East Germany before the fall of the Berlin Wall. Even the smell brings it back to me. Somewhere a furious painting of a soviet soldier jumping with his Kalashnikov at the ready over the dead body of a German soldier, a tank and a plane outlined against a steel blue sky. A yellowed newspaper, a door nailed shut. I suddenly think of the Japanese *mono no aware*, which expresses the same idea as the title of a book by Dimitri Verhulst: the sadness of things. When I look out through the grimy windows, I see the vast industrial complex of the mine, rusty cranes, empty sheds, pipelines climbing up the grey-brown hill, gas tanks now useless, idle forklift trucks, and all this against the backdrop of nature ready to reclaim her territory. "Bar," "Museum" is written in red letters on two signs mounted on a yellow-brick wall, but what exactly did that represent?

Nearly 1,500 people lived in this closed enclave, so many hours of sail from the only other inhabited spot. There was even a (Norwegian) post office; its placard hangs next to an English map: "Farm," "Canteen," "Hospital," "Office," "Landing Ground." What is left of the interiors already belongs itself in a museum … the deserted canteen, chairs coated with the debris of decay. Outside stands the wooden sculpture of a small tower topped by a hammer and sickle. Above these are stylized red and white flames silhouetted against the mountain of waste as though cut out with a fret saw. Also, in front of the main building looms a tall round sign with the name of the company, Arktikugol. It depicts the uppermost part of an ice blue globe inscribed with the number 79, the degree of latitude we are at, above two crossed hammers. Over the Pole, drawn as a tiny circle, floats the red soviet star. The whole tableau is crowned with a huge polar bear. The soviet star no longer exists, but the dream symbolized by the drawing lingers on – somewhere under that massive wilderness of ice the new Russia has staked its claims. When we walk back between our armed protectors, I see the head of Lenin whose gaze sweeps over the top of the vacant buildings of his abandoned colony and fixes on the distant icebergs. Chin jutting out, piercing eyes, I haven't gone yet, and don't you forget it. Perhaps I will be called Putin next, or Medvedev, or Gazprom, or simply Russia again, because what all of you thought was ice is actually protruding land, extending far into the Arctic Ocean, and that land is ours, along with everything that goes with it.

IV. On the following days we travel to Hammerfest and Kirkenes, an old desire. Always peered at those endless roads through Norway, never thought I would get there like this. Rome is closer to Oslo than Hammerfest, someone tells me. Hammerfest, the world's northernmost town: on the day we arrive it's dull and grey, but a flame seems to light up the whole bay. This is a gas and oil capital. Part of Norway's immense wealth originates right here. We get a crash course on how it all works. We see the marble column erected in 1854 to commemorate the first measurement of the earth. Then we can watch from behind glass how men and women from the four corners of the globe gut fish for the whole world at a conveyor belt to earn money to support entire families on other continents.

The last town we visit is Kirkenes, where street names are marked in both Norwegian and Russian. It lies just as far east as Istanbul, as far from Oslo as Oslo from Rome. Murmansk is close by. Russian ships are repaired here. Rusty and battered they lie moored in the harbour where icy winds prevail. Later, at the library, the entwining is even more noticeable: half the book collection consists of Russian volumes, and the Russian librarian makes a speech that is translated into English by her Norwegian colleague. Four hundred women live in Kirkenes, and in the perpetually dark winter months a lot of reading is done. There are only a few streets – *frontier* the Americans would call this, border territory, adventure territory. The seamen's club, cars with Russian license plates, and towering above everything the tall monument the Norwegians built for the Russian soldiers who in 1944 helped liberate Norway. What isn't inscribed on the monument is that the Russians themselves didn't leave right away either, rather like visitors who were warmly welcomed for tea but ended up staying a bit too long. Here, as on Spitsbergen, fighting was fierce. Kirkenes was attacked from the air more than three hundred times, and when the Germans left, they burned the town so completely all that remained was scorched earth.

v. Of the collection of maps I still have of this trip, the one of the last day is the most beautiful. It is called "Grense Jakobselv." The map is almost completely blue, but through all that blue runs a pink line with crosses, Russian water on one side, Norwegian on the other. There is also a tiny bit of land on it, but without settlements of any kind, only shadings indicating elevations and hollows, and figures are printed in inland waterways that sometimes have a name. A white land, a wild land. We drive there from Kirkenes along Road 886. After Bjornstad the road no longer has a number. The river beside us is the border. On our side, the border posts are yellow; the Russian ones across the water are red and green. The exact line of the frontier runs along the river's deepest channel. The land looks boggy. Squat shrubs with orange-red berries, Siberian chives, dough-coloured fungi, flowers white and crimson, low green plants that look like glasswort. On the coast itself the cliffs are slate grey, worn smooth, full of cracks and grooves, the script of the sea. The Cold War is history, but not for those who witnessed it all. Budapest 1956, Berlin 1953, Berlin 1989 – I have stood plenty of times in a place where the two systems met, and it's much the same here, although those days are long gone. In the desolation to the right I see the Russians barracks where the border patrol soldiers lived, and a little further away, on top of the cliffs, the tall watch towers. To the left, on the Norwegian side, NATO's listening post, "where they could pick up every sound."

It is probably just imagination, but something of the menace of those days is still in the air. At the spot where the river flows into the sea, you look out at those now innocent buildings and the invisible border that used to spell death for whoever tried to escape across it. Nearby stands an earlier warning, King Oscar II's chapel dating from 1869, a rugged building made of gneiss, a sign meant to make clear to the Russian neighbours just who was the boss here. When we come closer, a few cars stop for a Sami wedding, women in traditional costume, men in black suits, the true inhabitants of these regions, who could once roam without worrying about frontiers, people of the Far North. Later I find in my notebook the border area's code of conduct, which I copied from a sign by the sea. Non-Norwegians are not permitted to fish in the Pasvik River, and only those people who have been living in Norway for a year and still do so are allowed to fish in the river in front of us, the Grense Jakob. Navigation is only permitted for boats with registration plates issued by the Norwegian Border Commission, and never at night. It is prohibited to cross the borderline, to try to make contact with persons on the other side or act in an insulting manner towards them. It is also prohibited to photograph Russian military installations, material or personnel, or throw something across the border. Any attempts at violations will be punished as if they had succeeded. The line has to be drawn somewhere after all.

III
Passage to Pyramiden

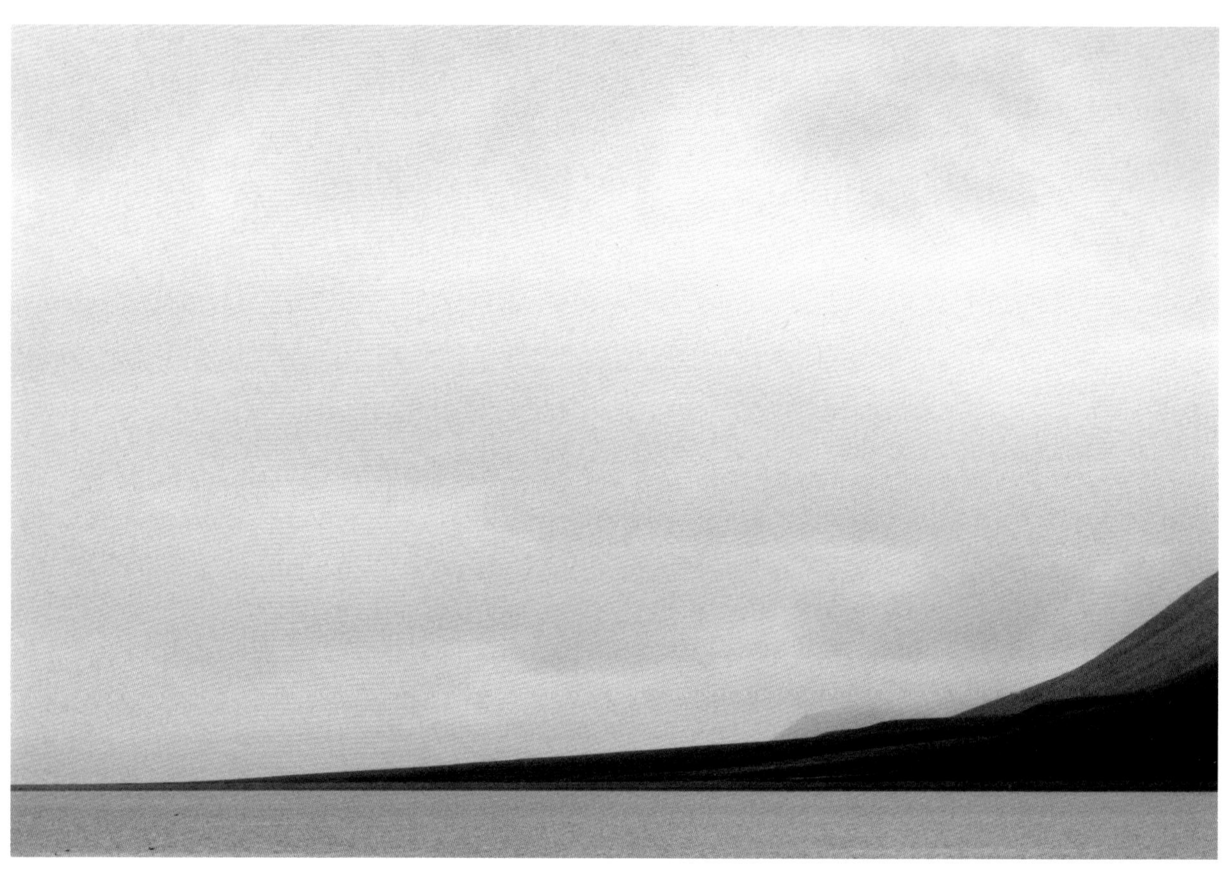

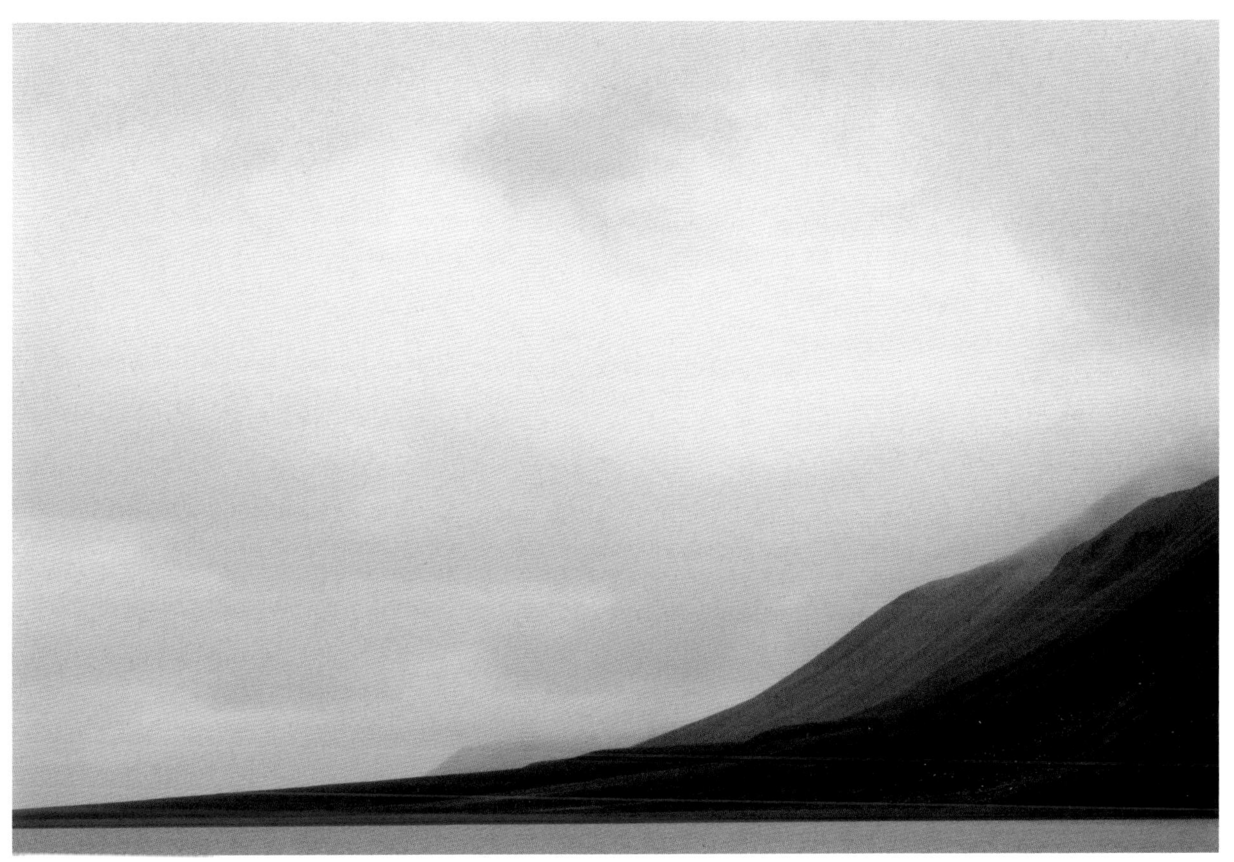

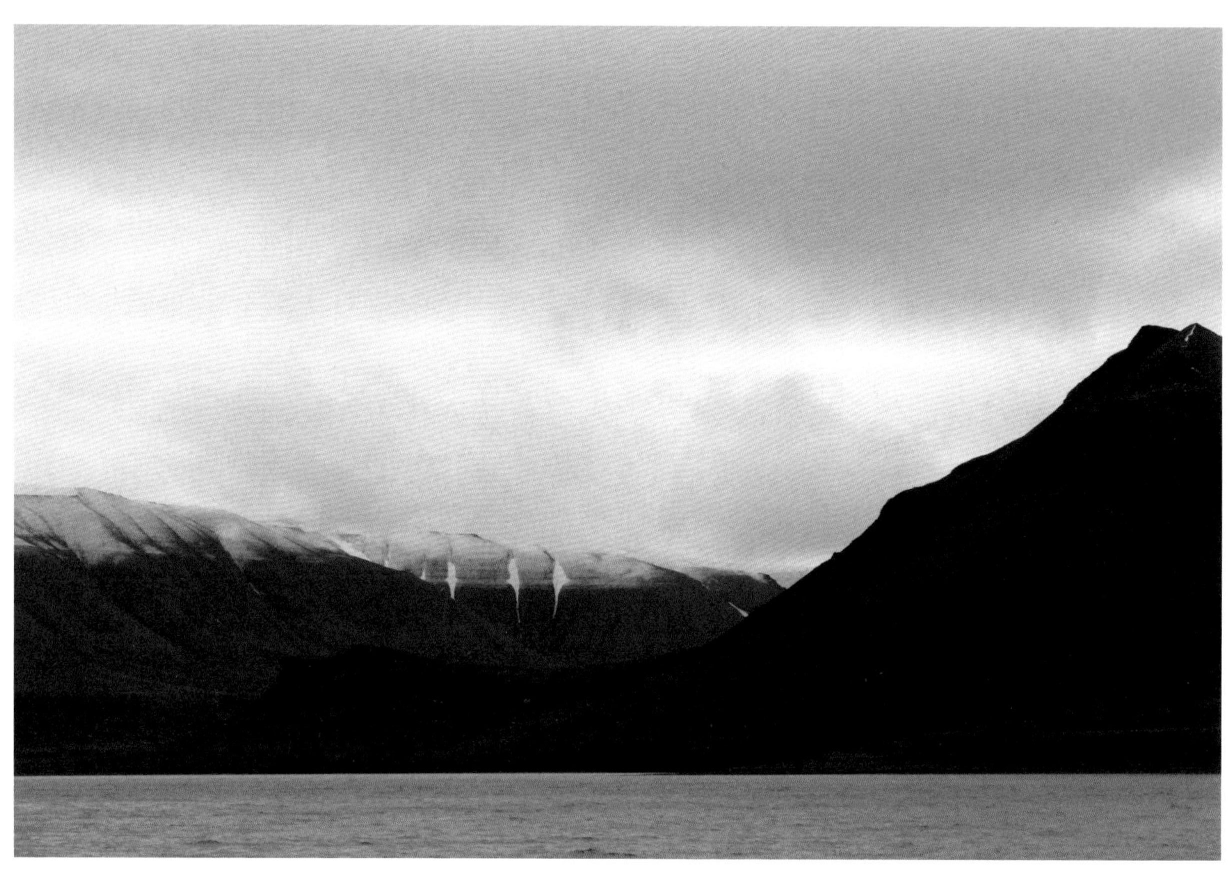

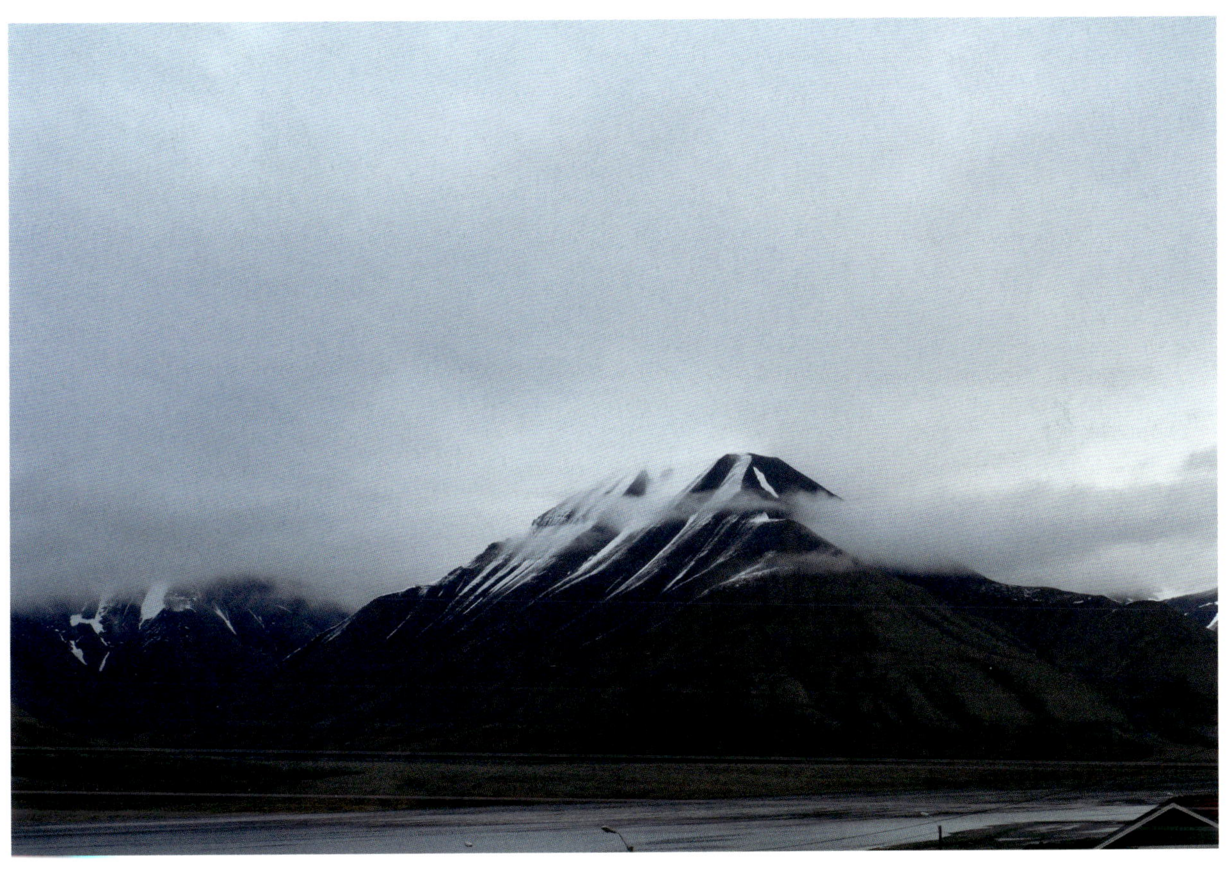

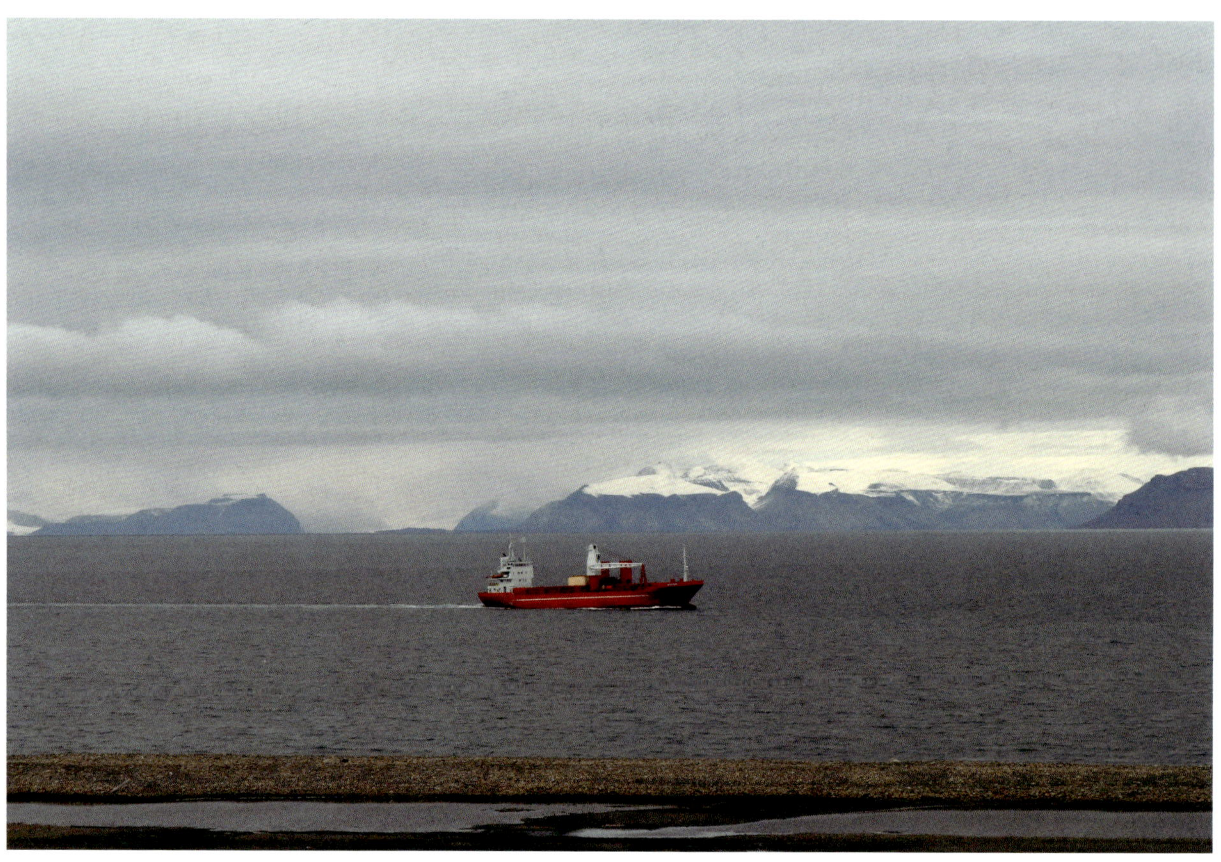

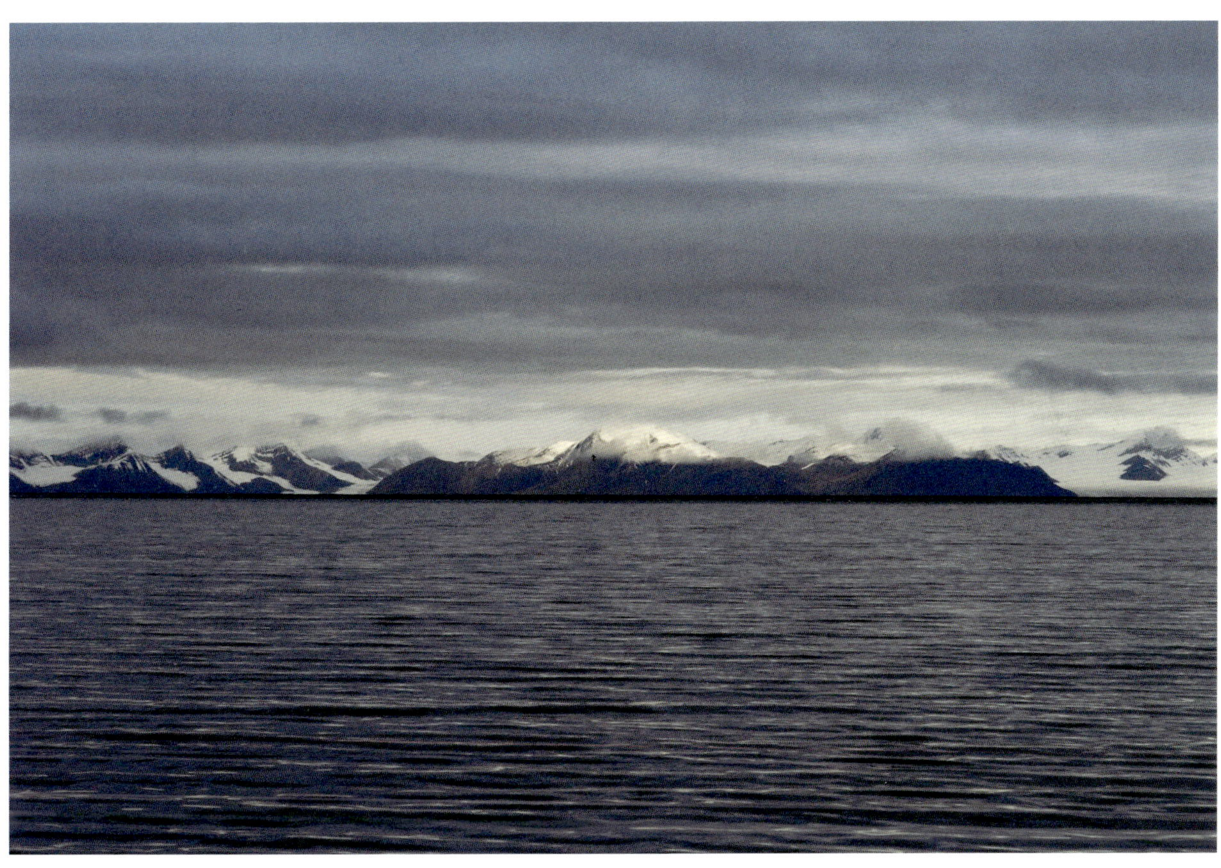

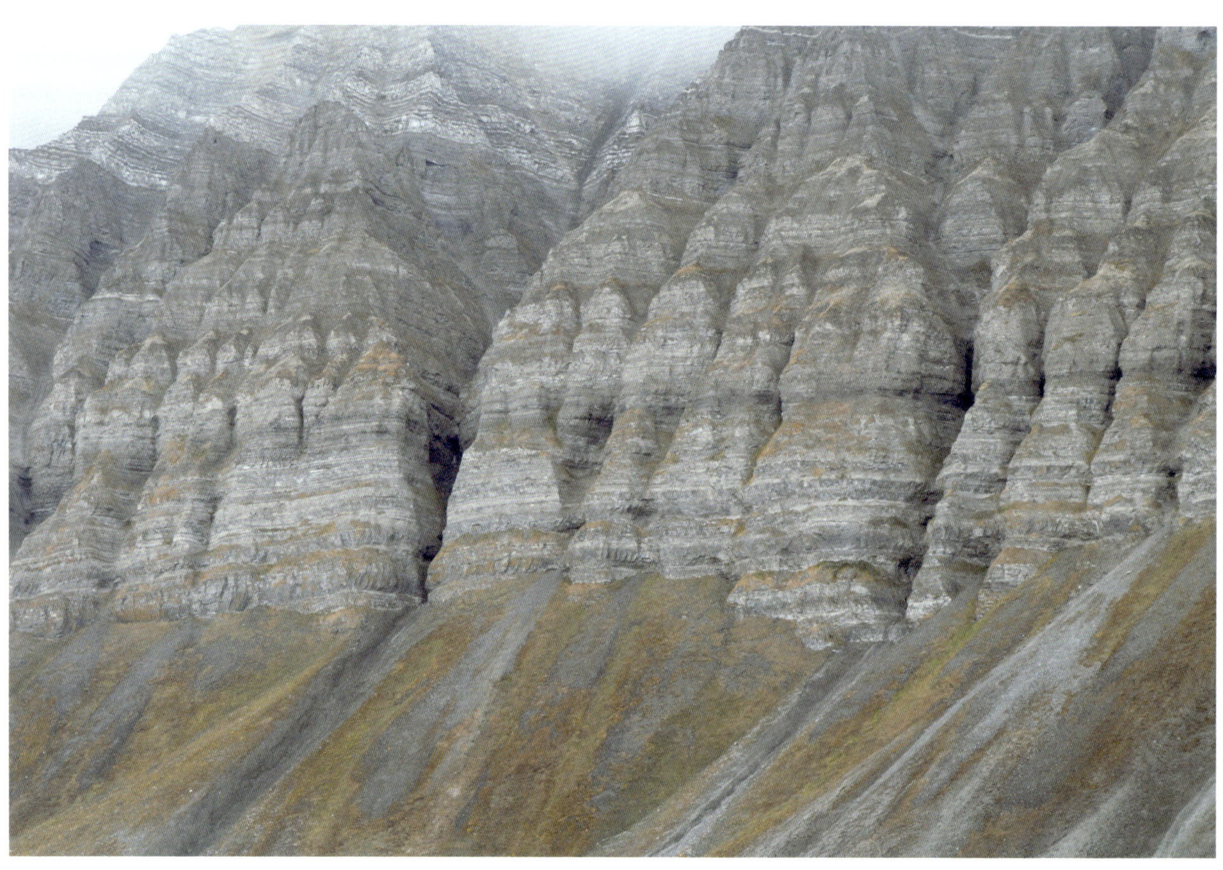

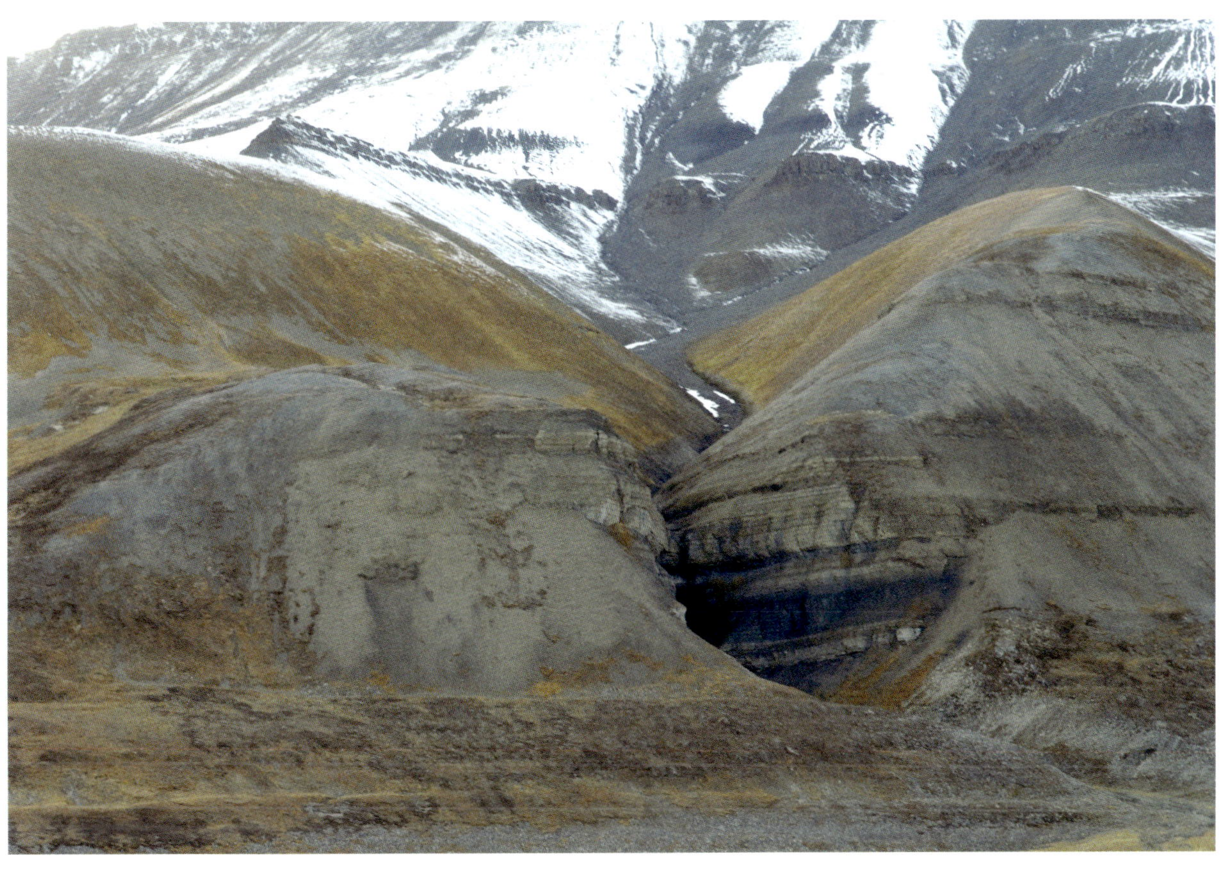

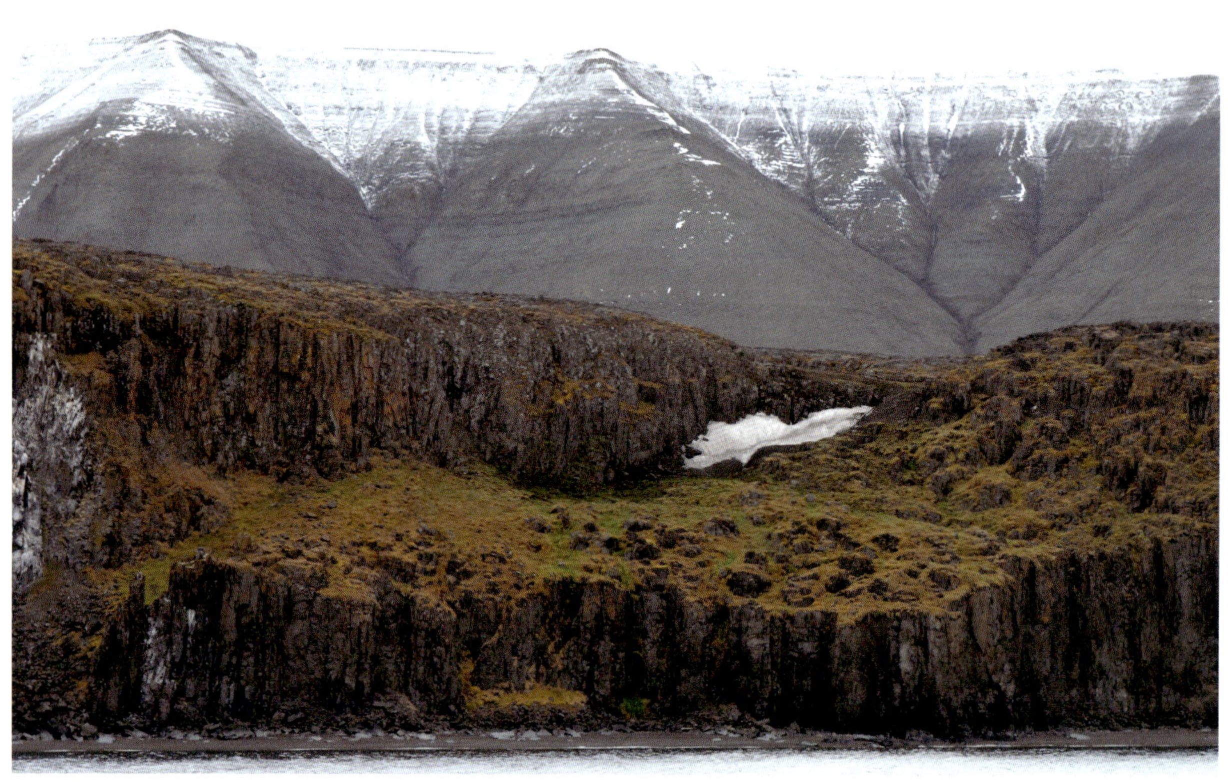

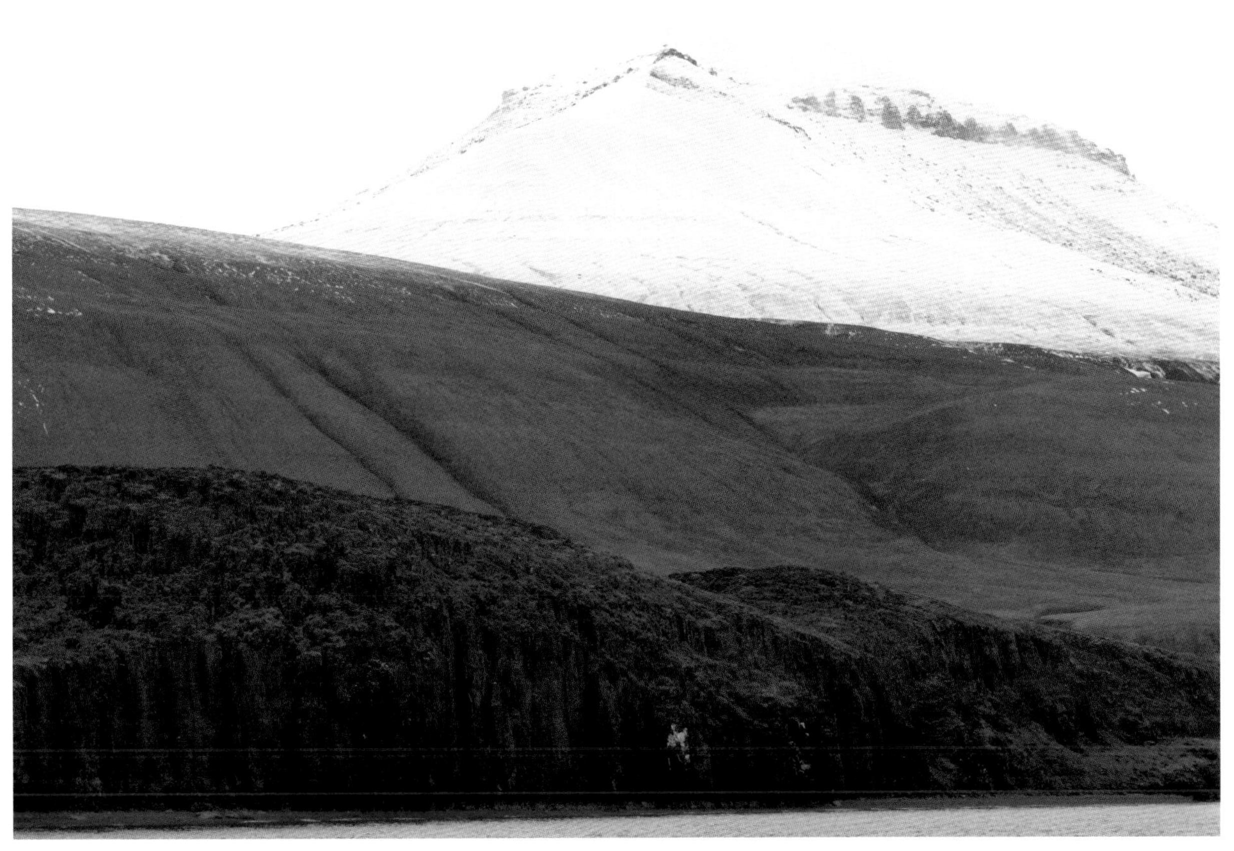

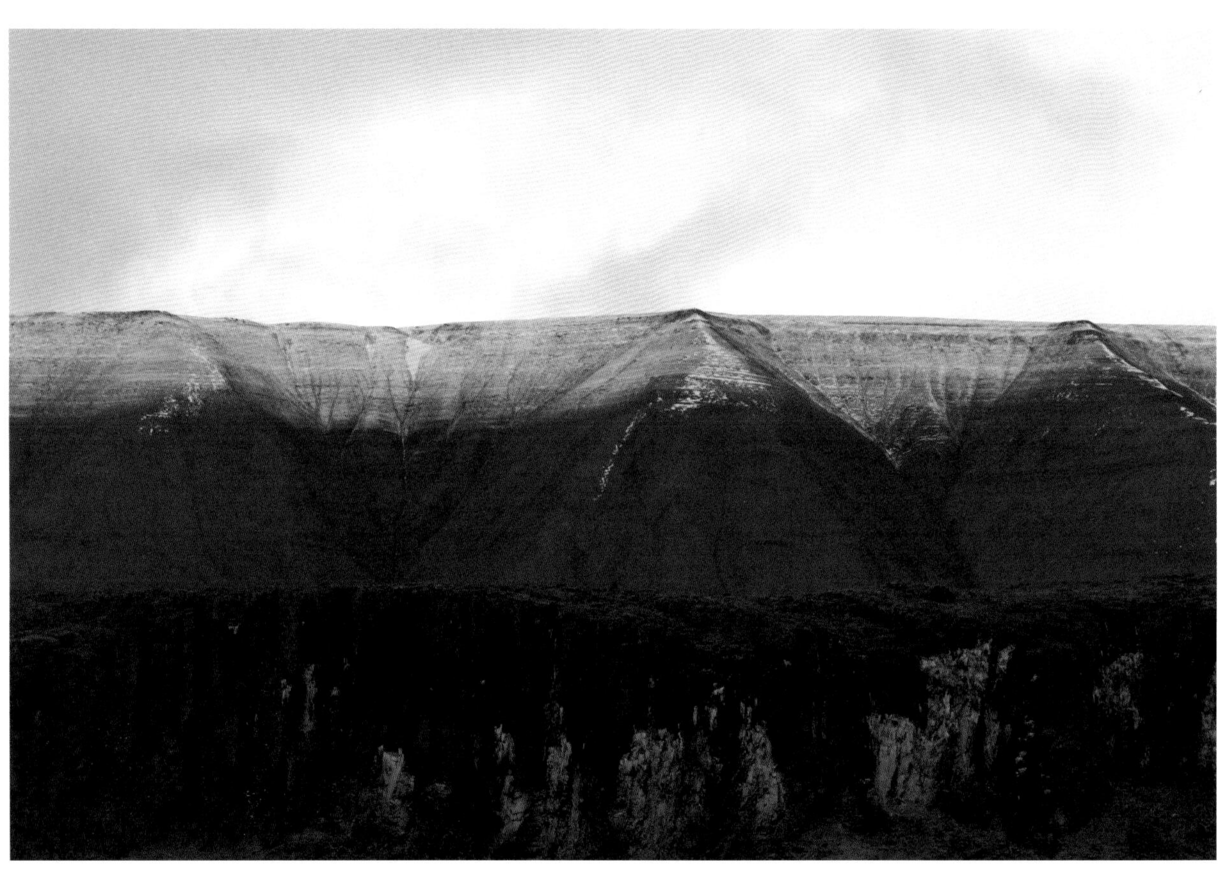

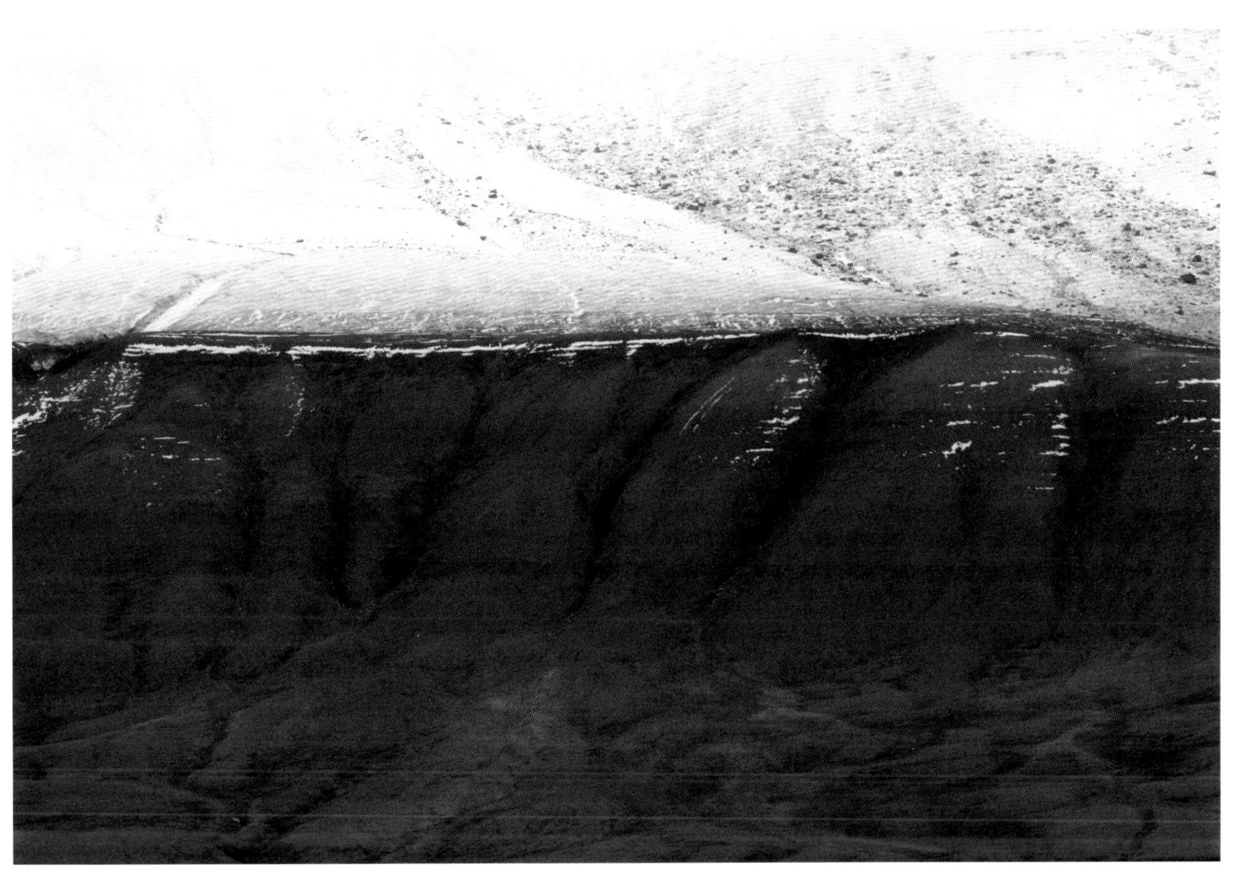

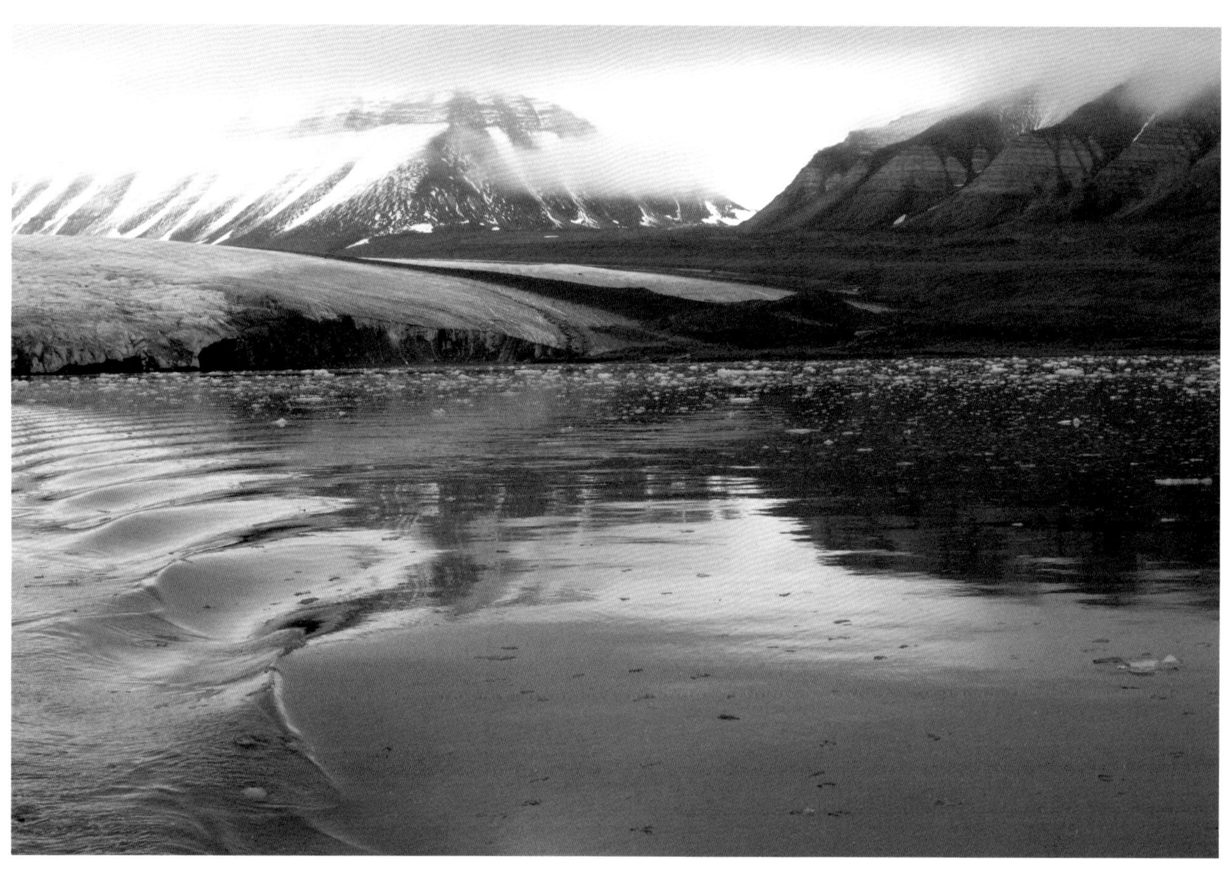

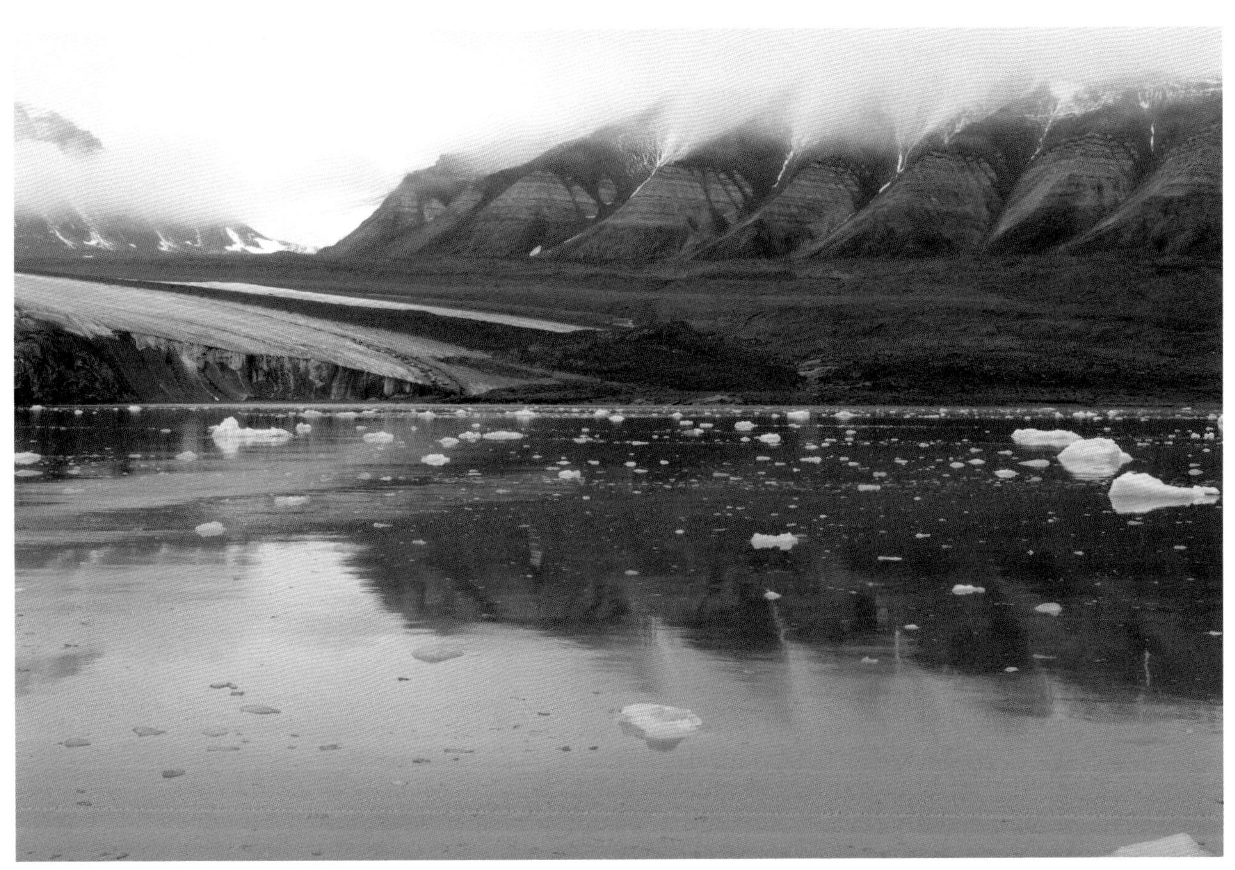

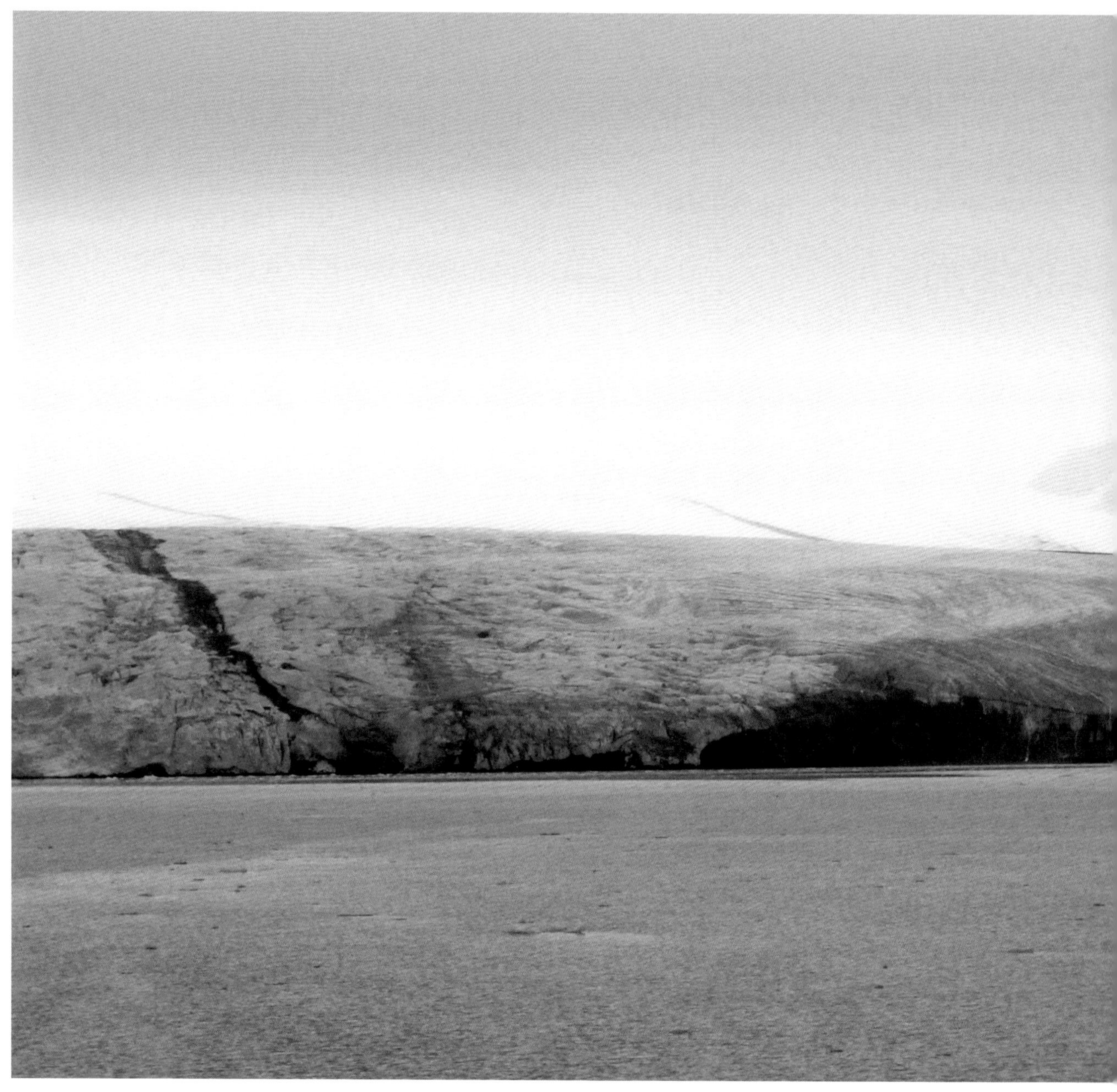

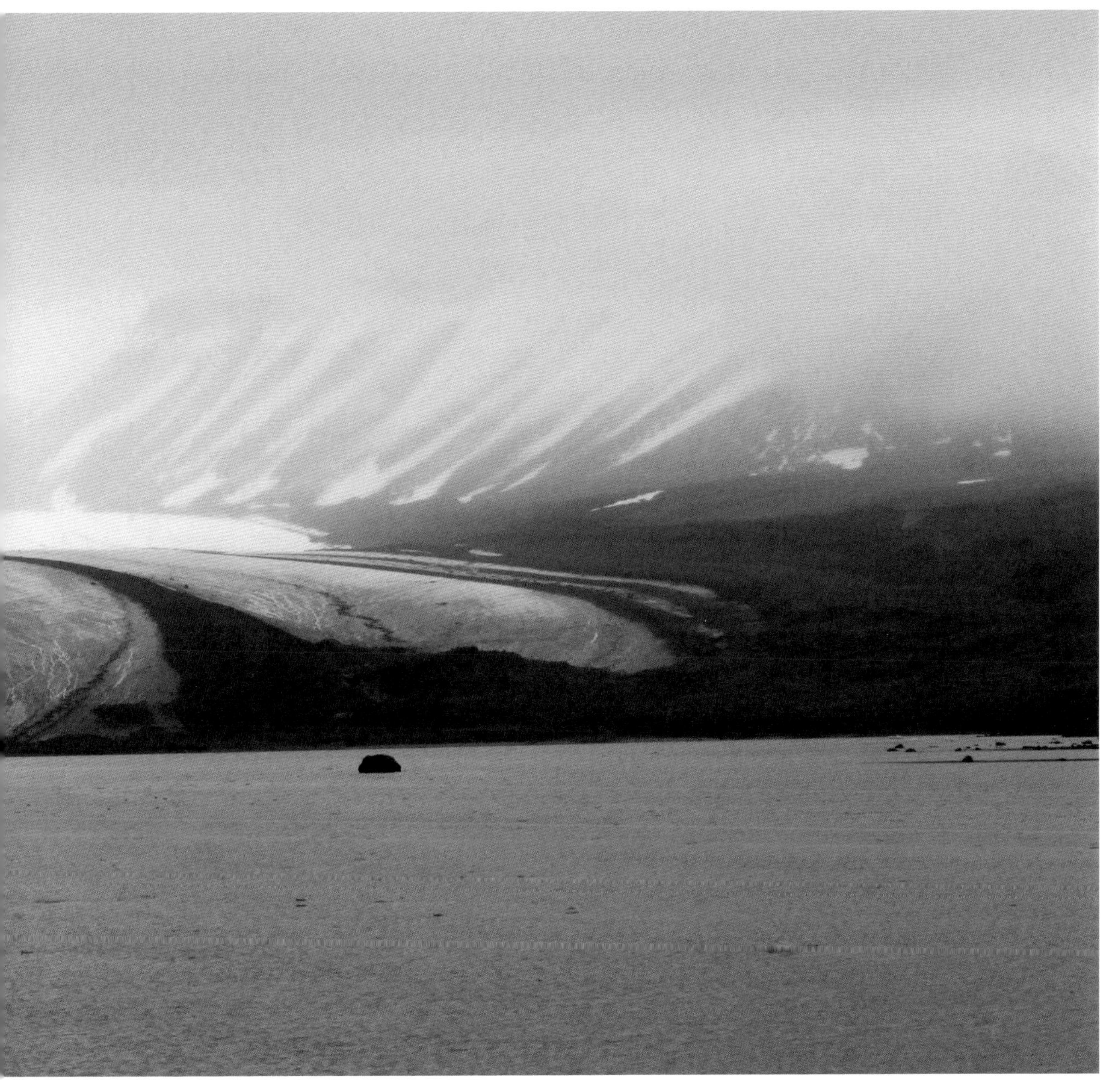

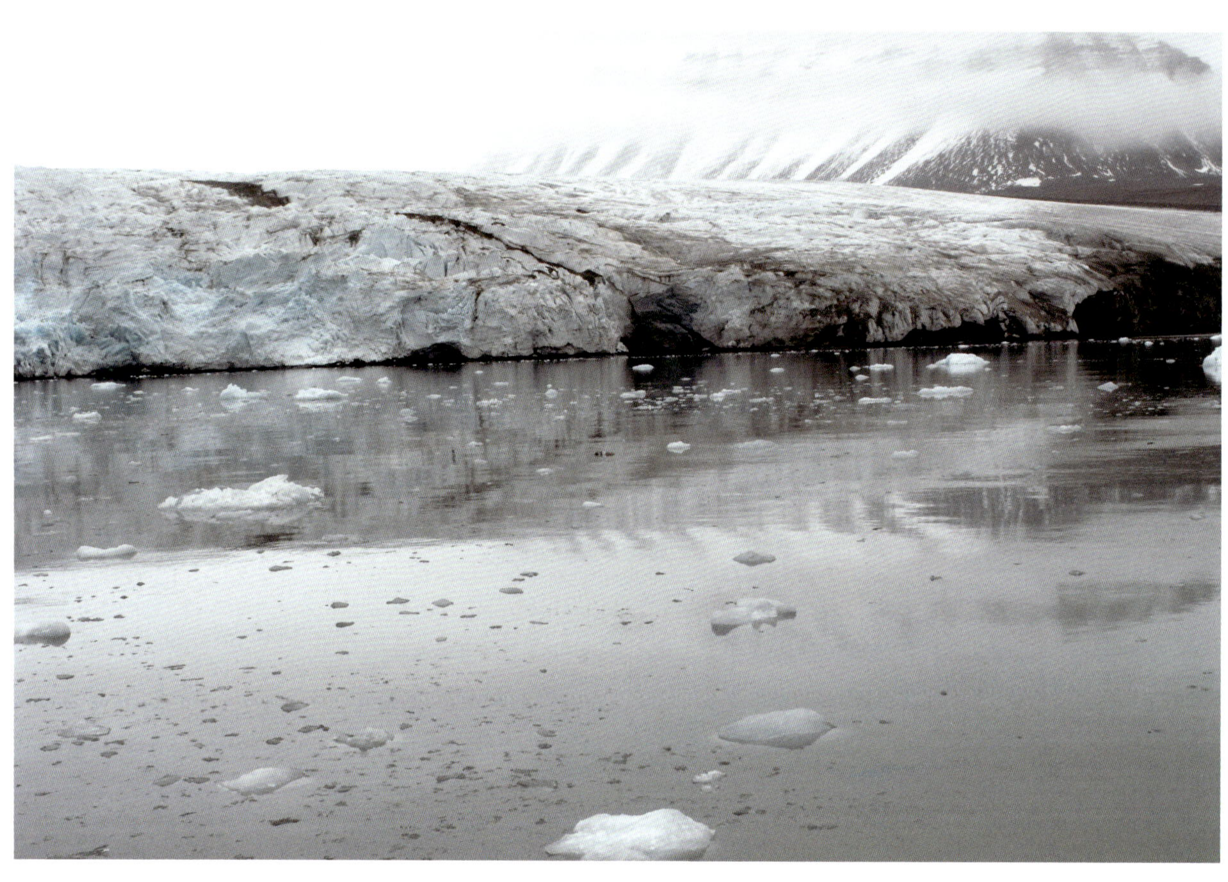

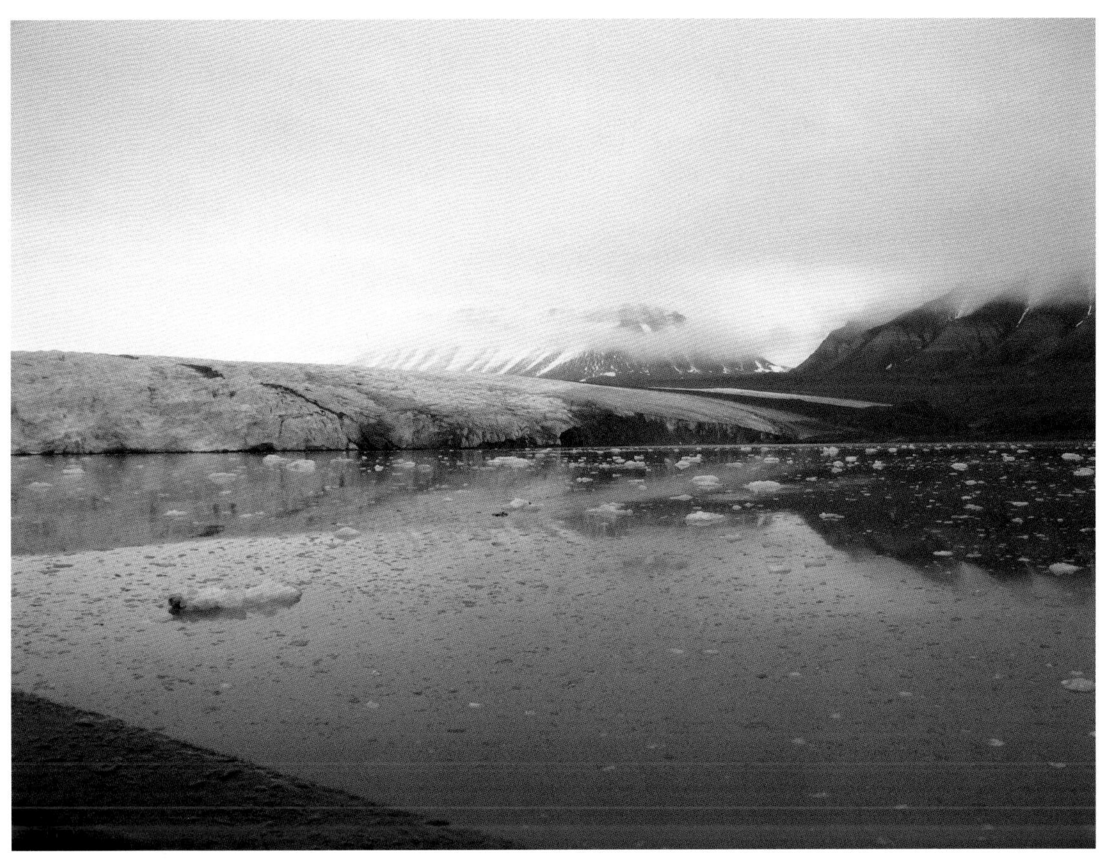

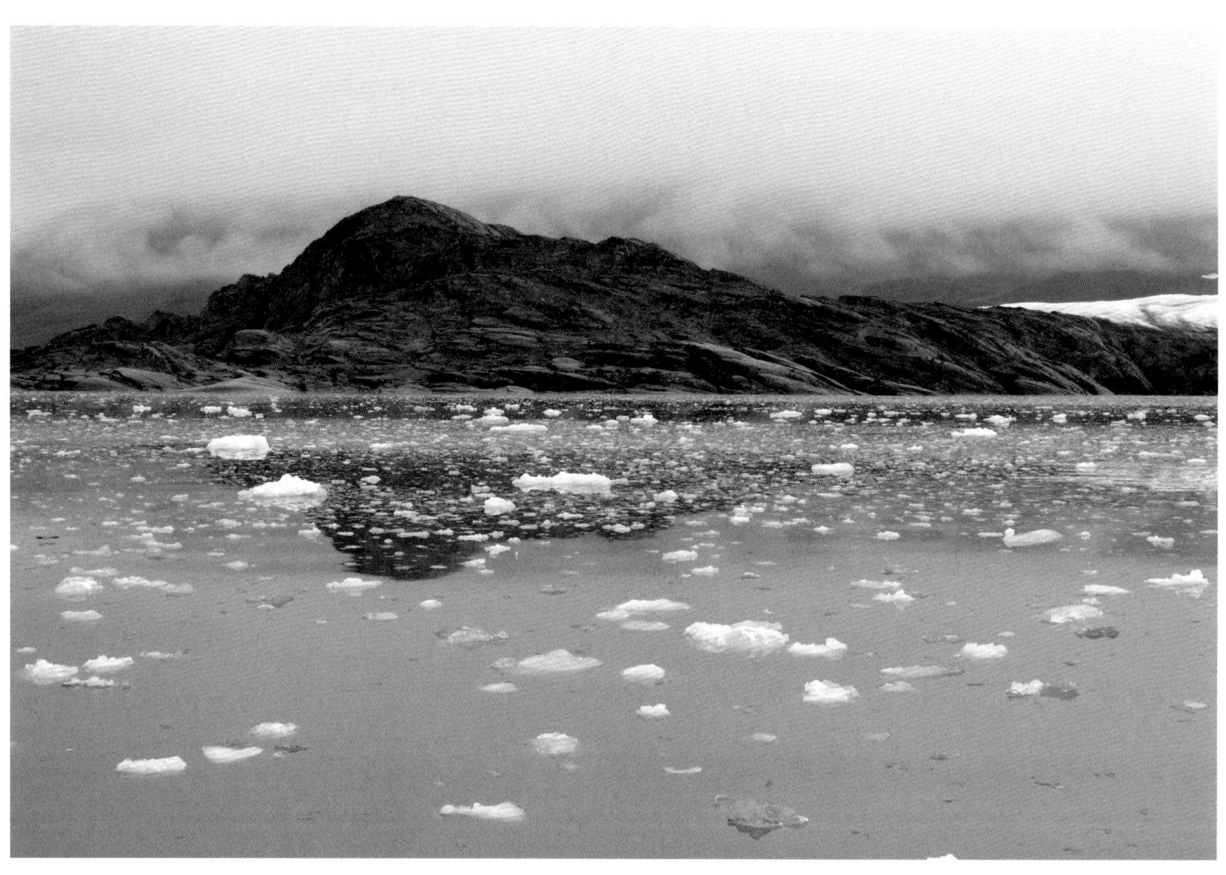

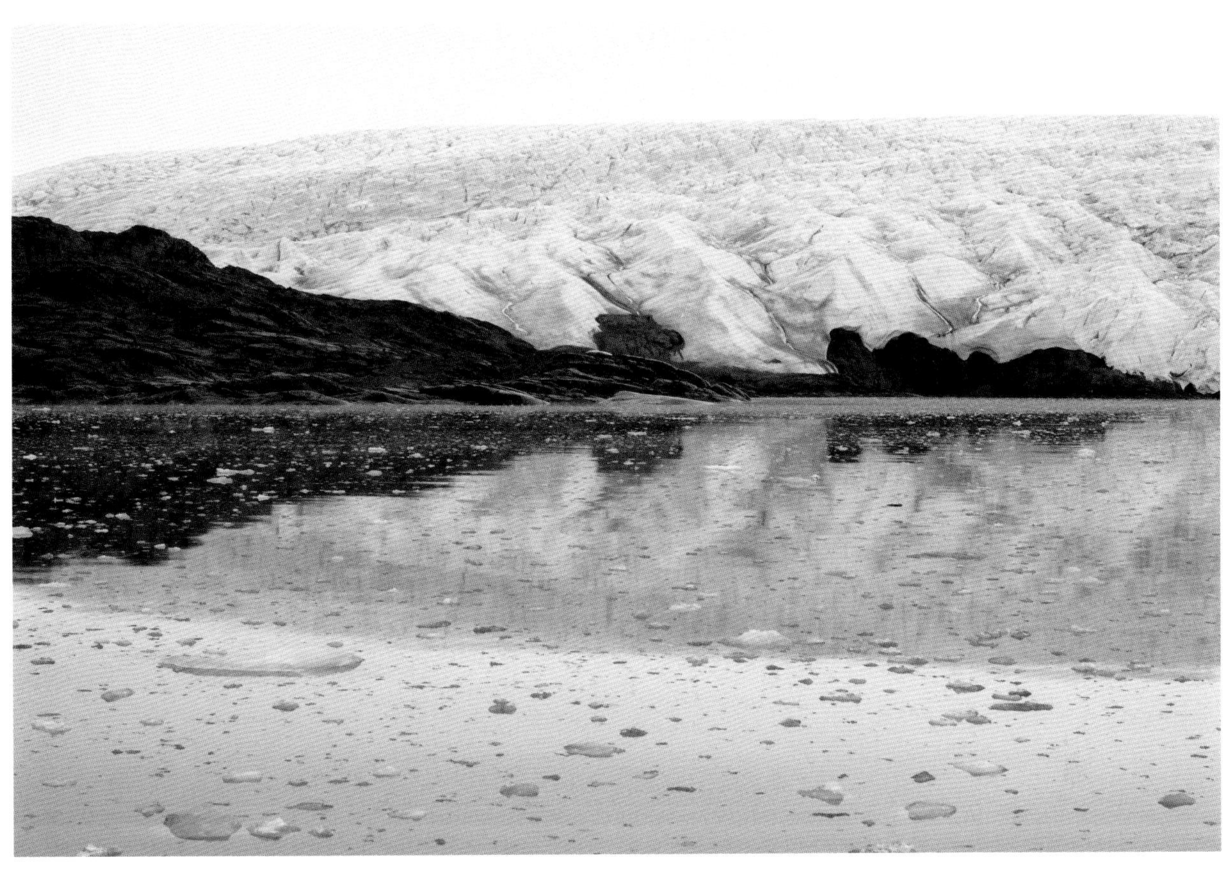

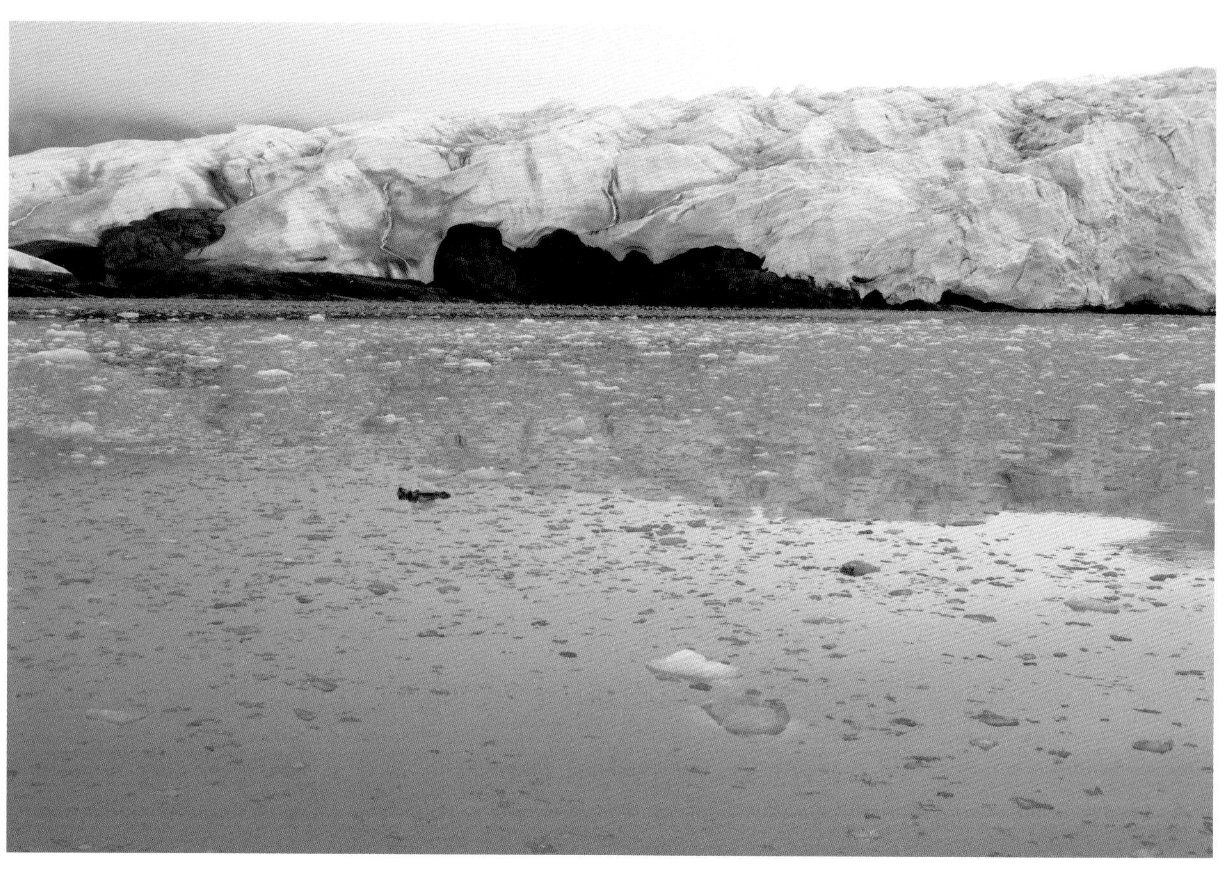

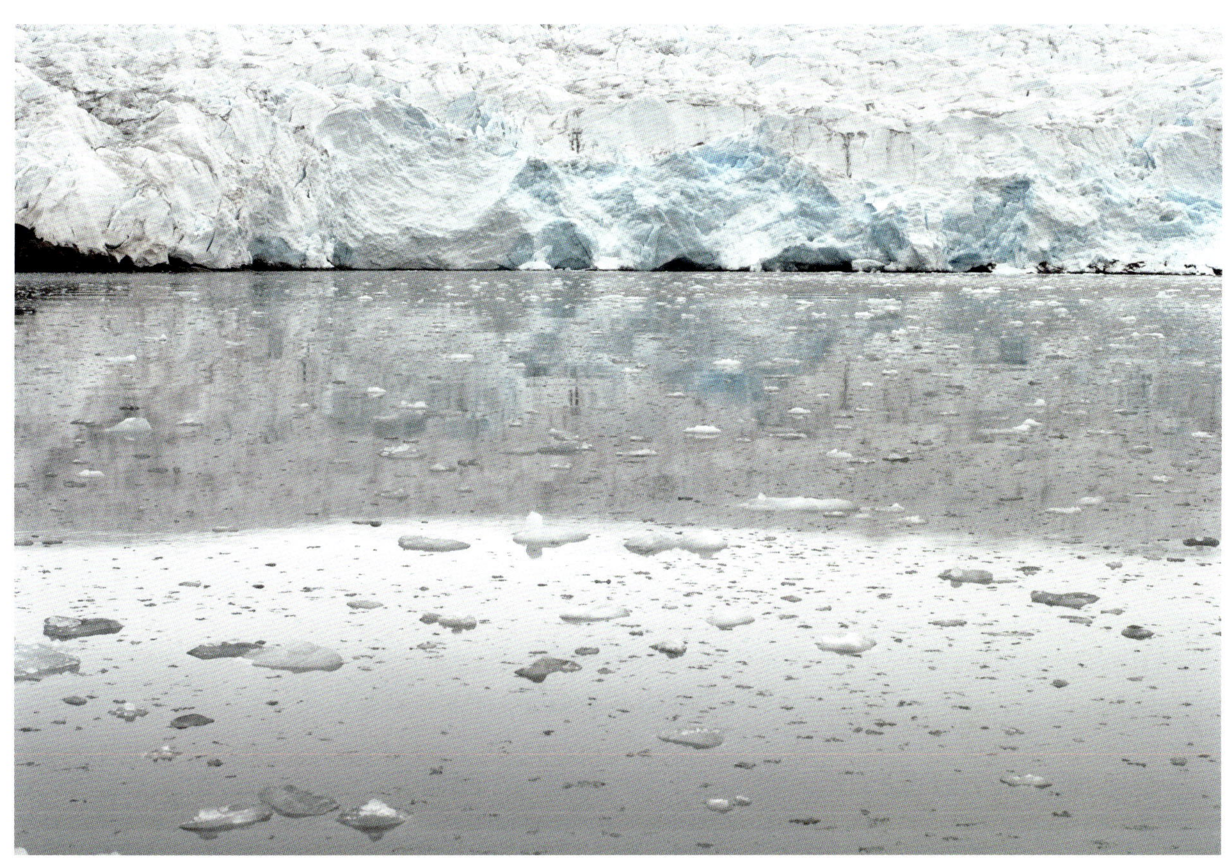

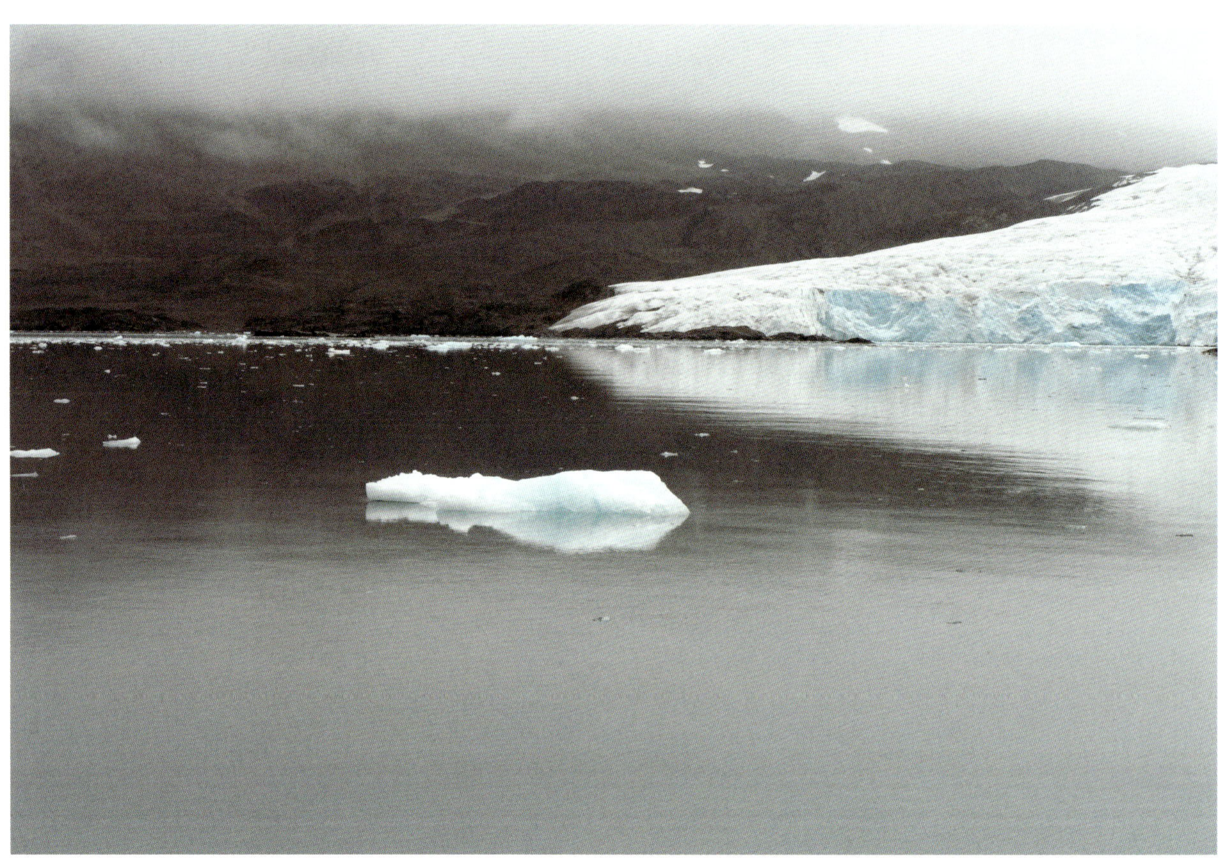

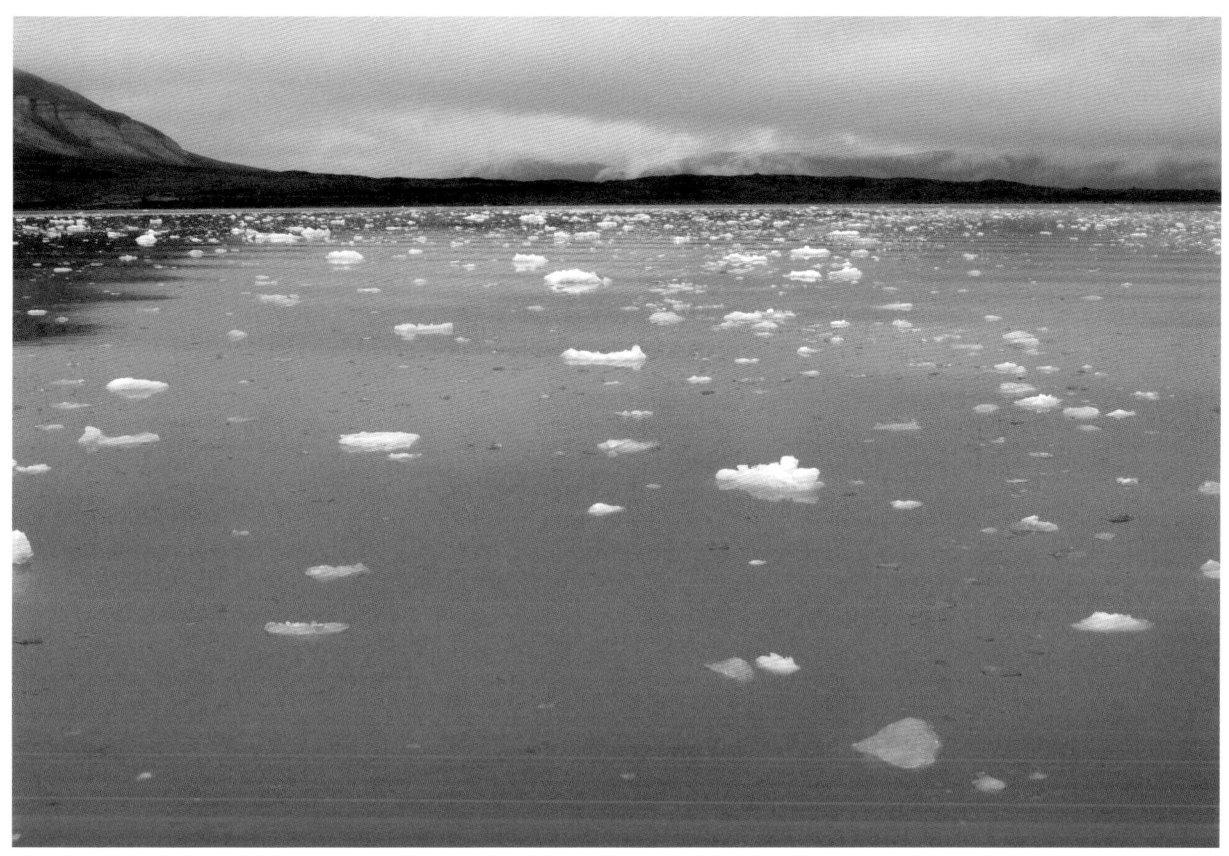

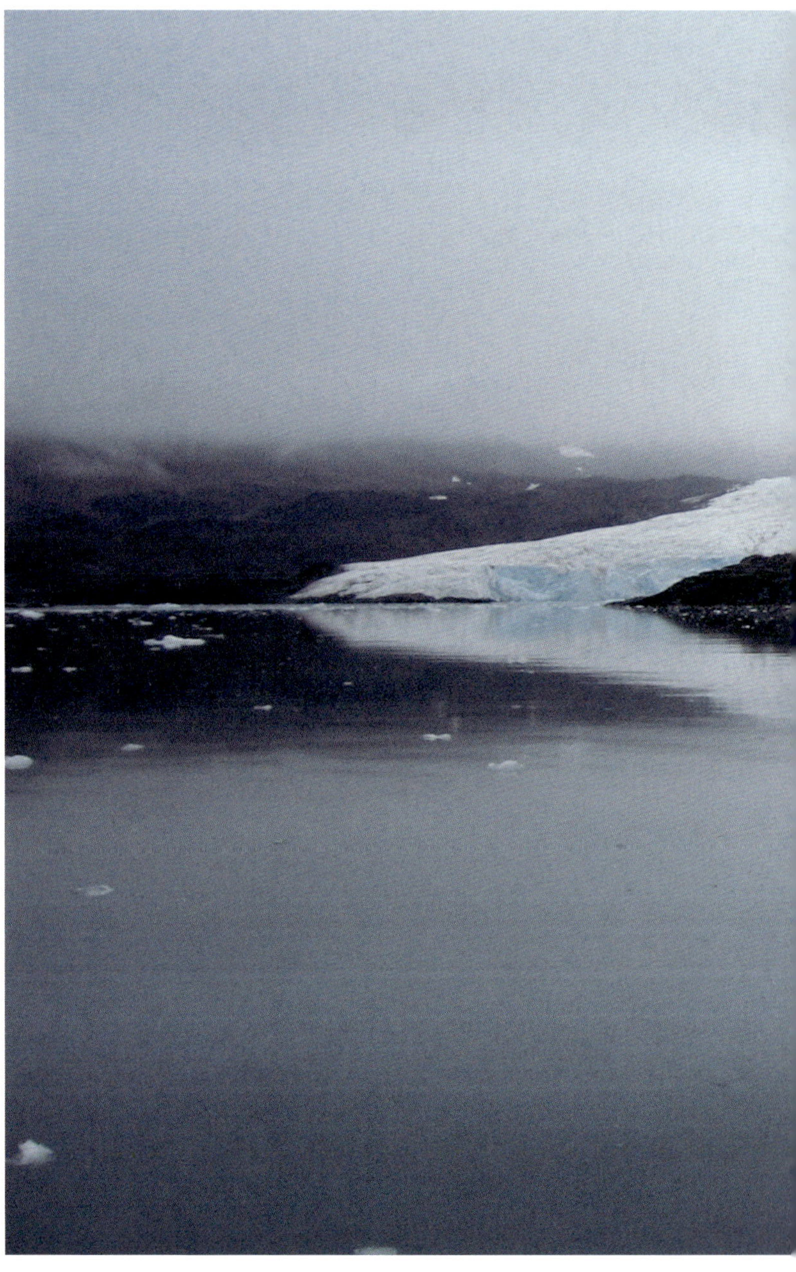

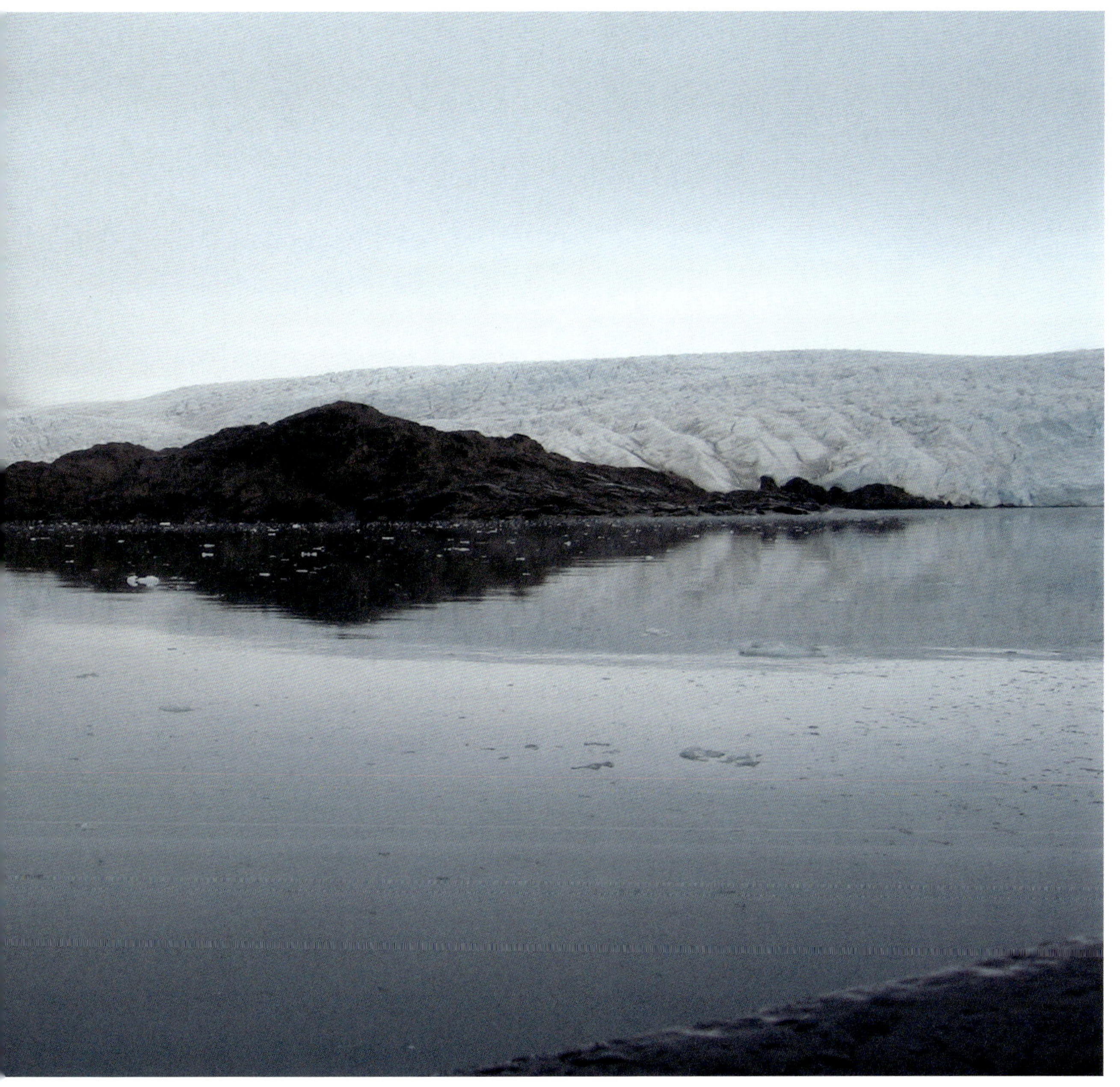

IV

In the Abandoned Mining Town of Pyramiden

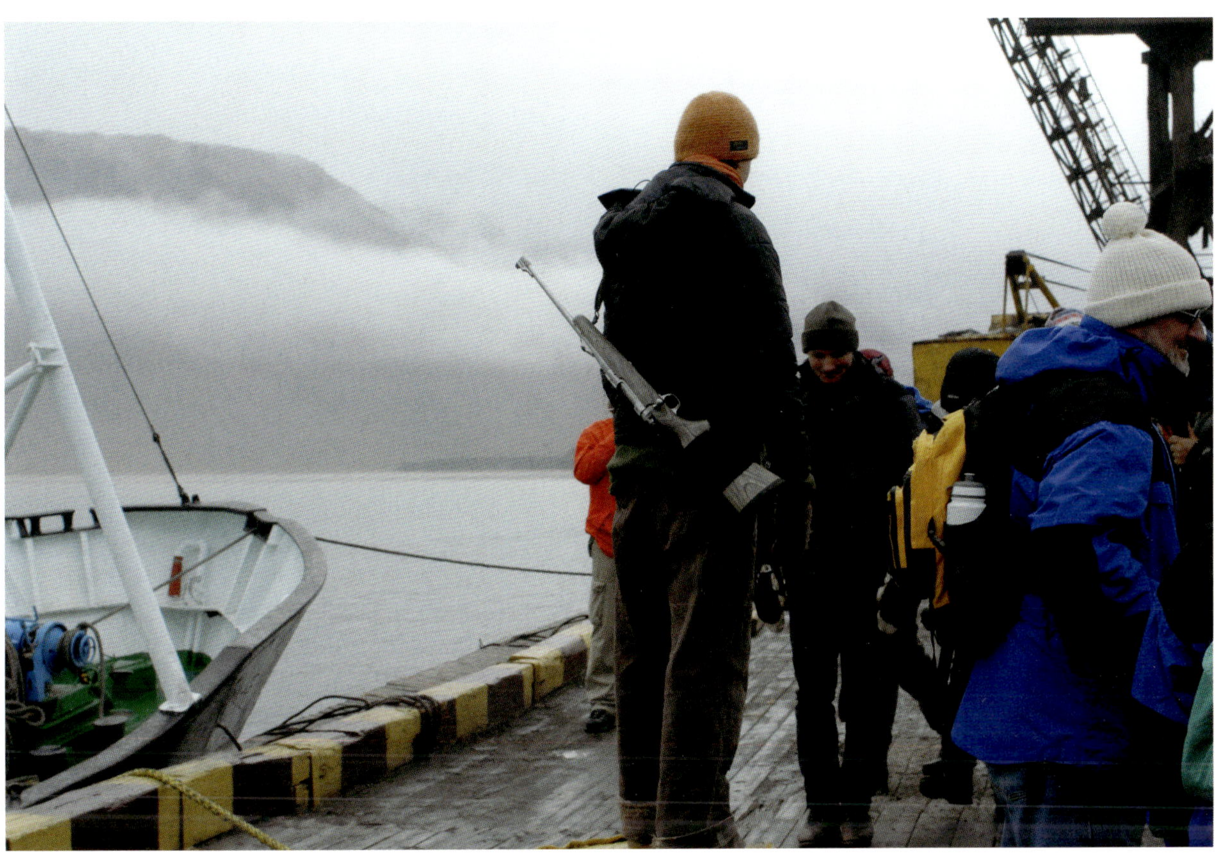

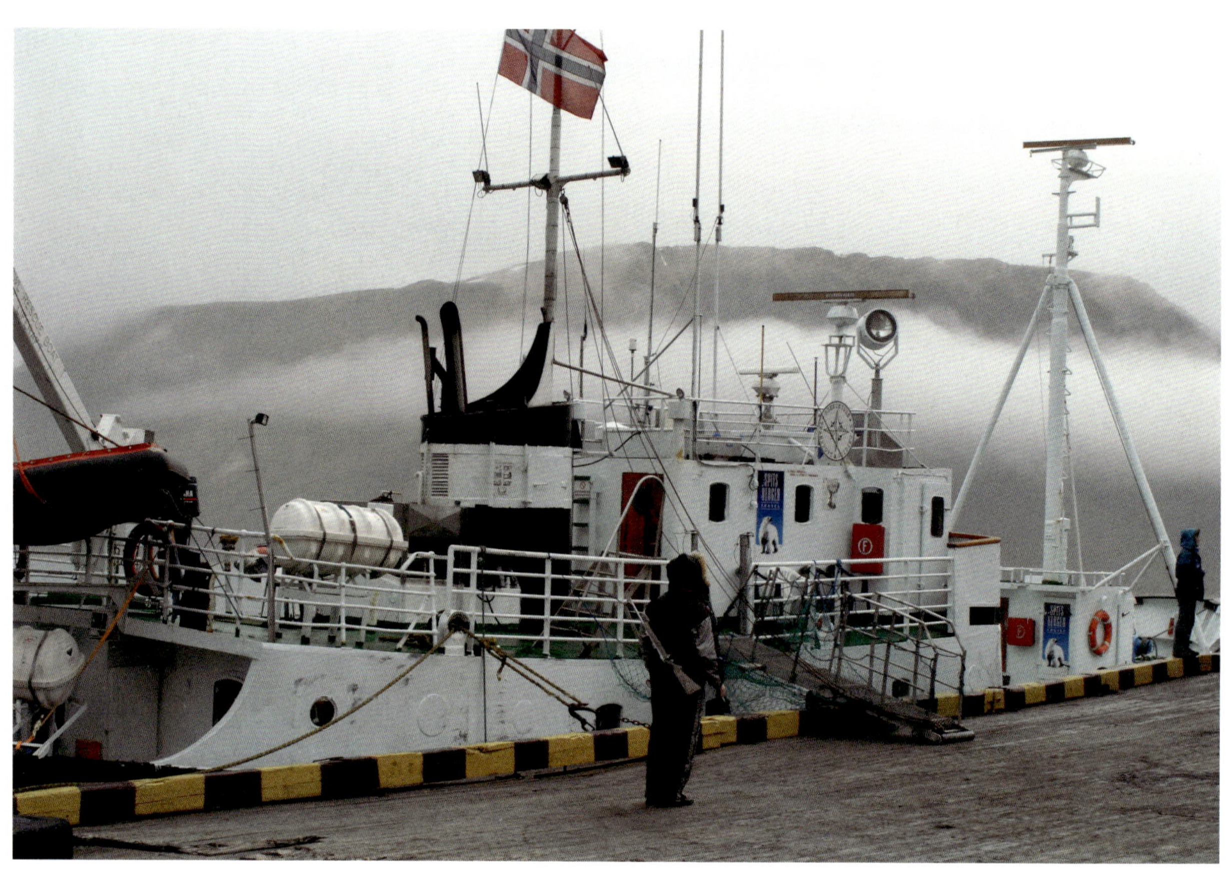

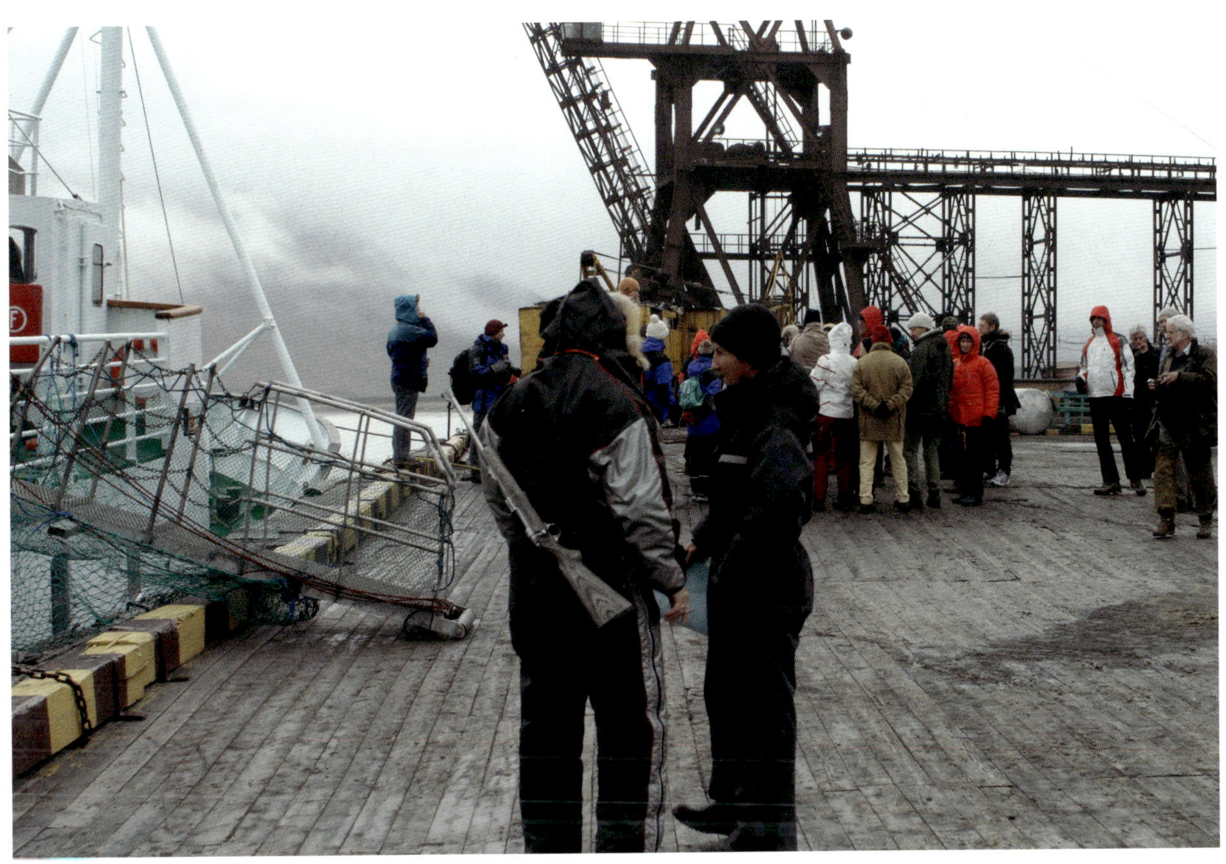

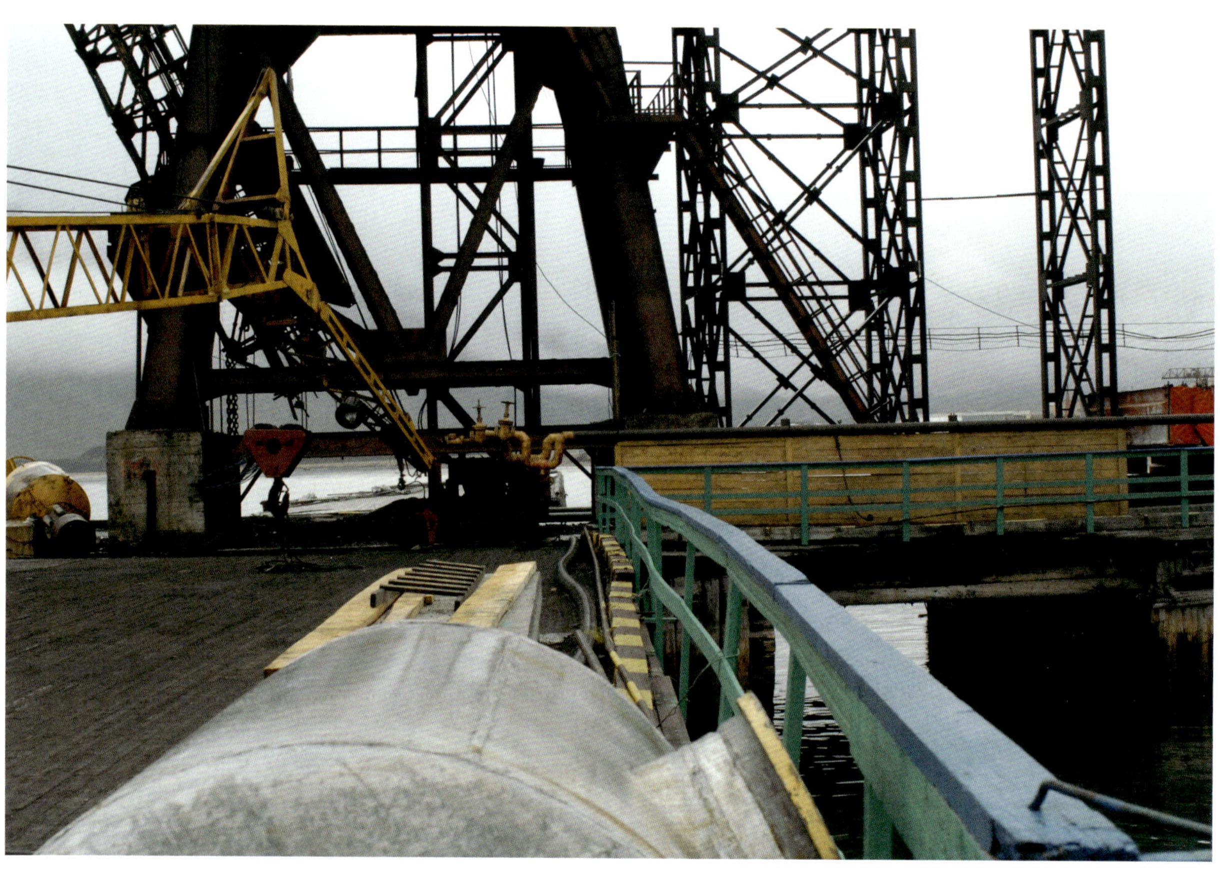

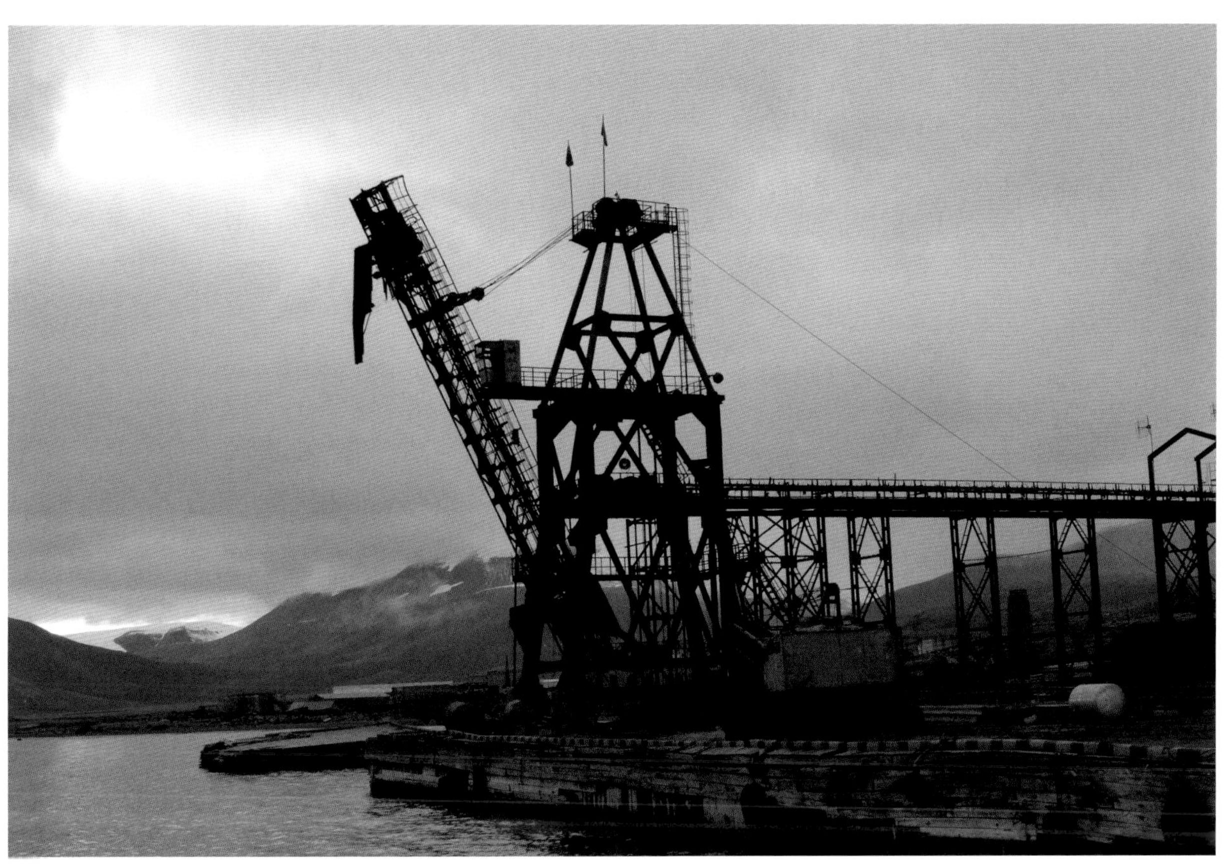

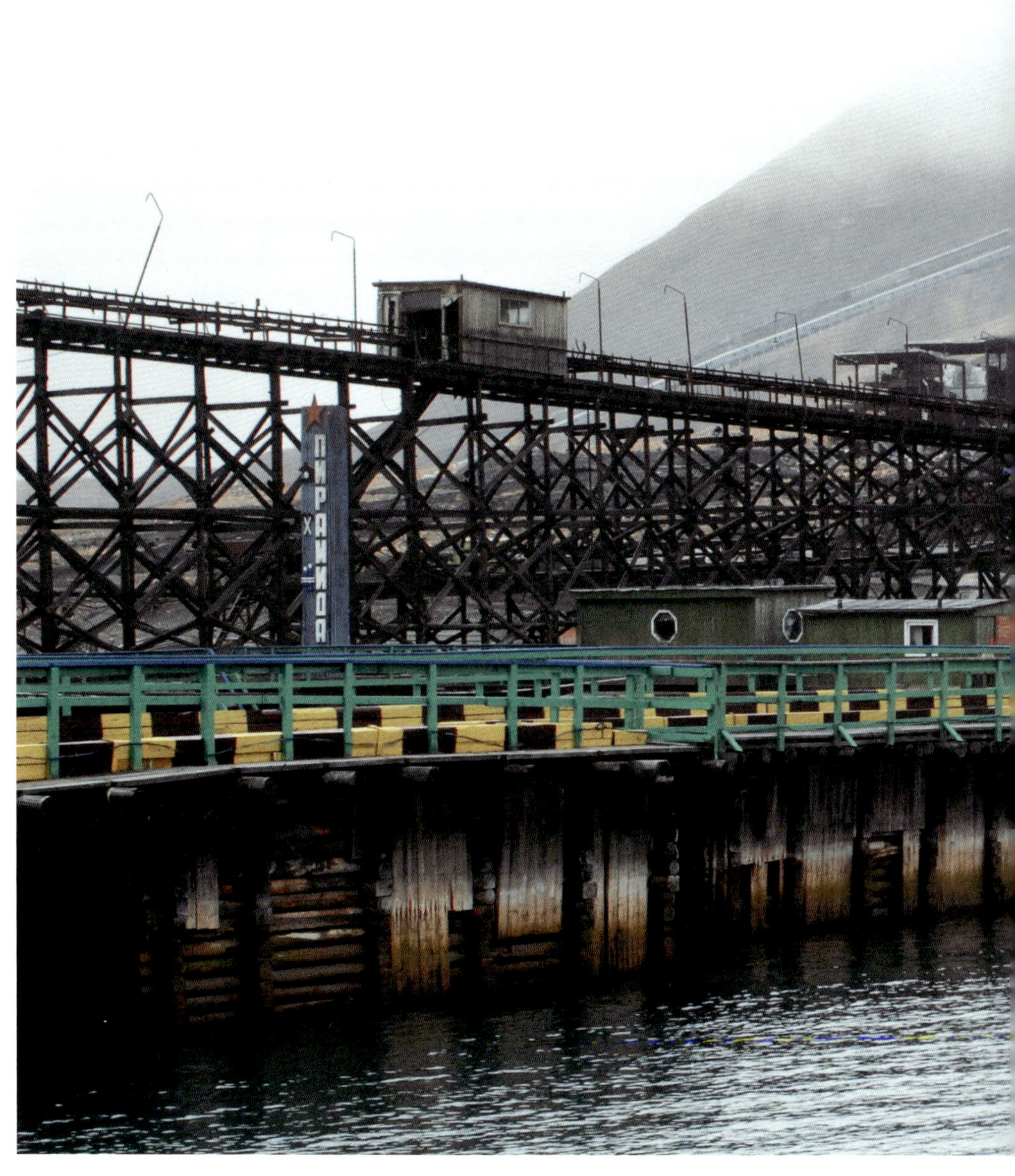
ПИРАМИДА

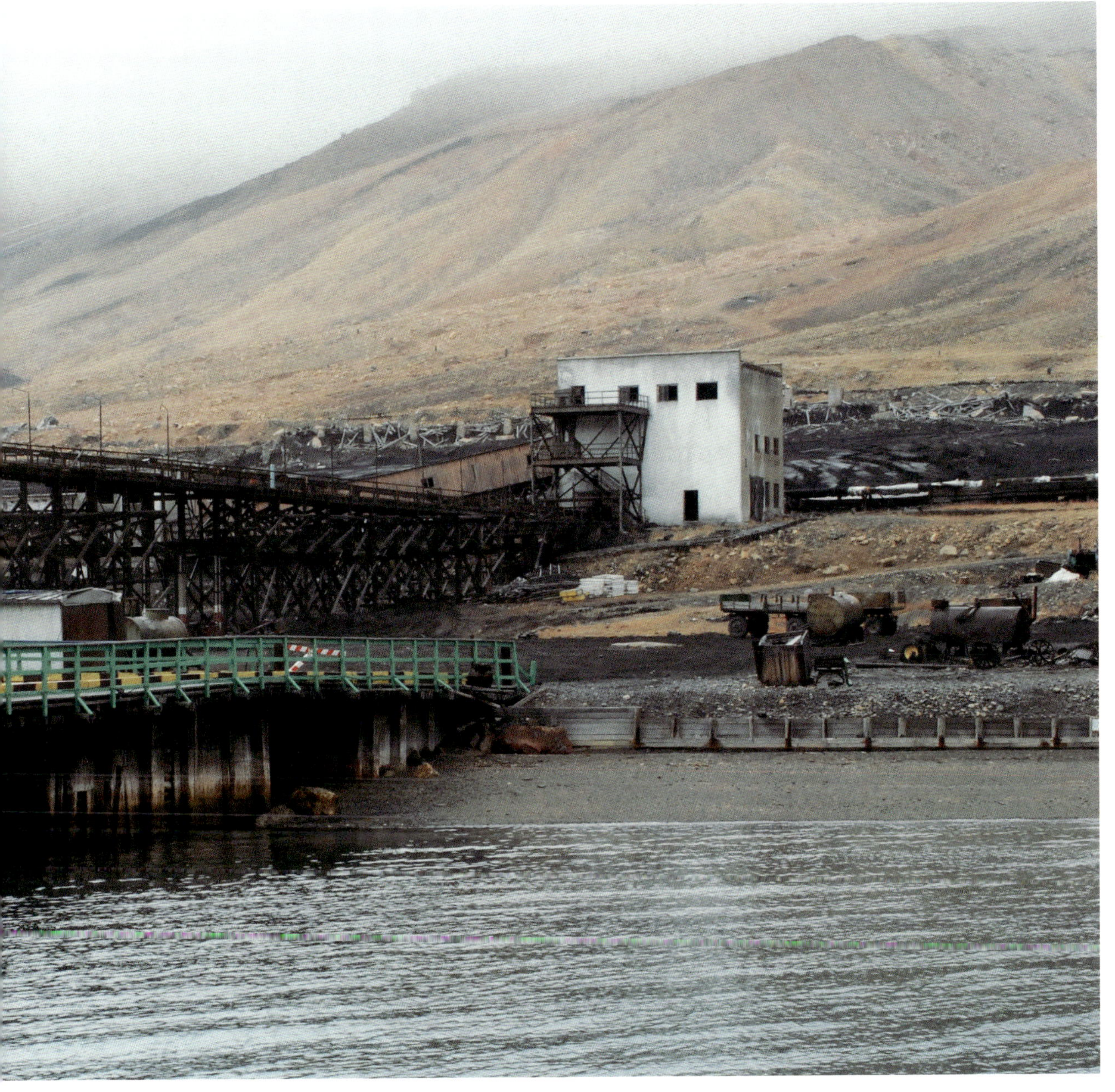

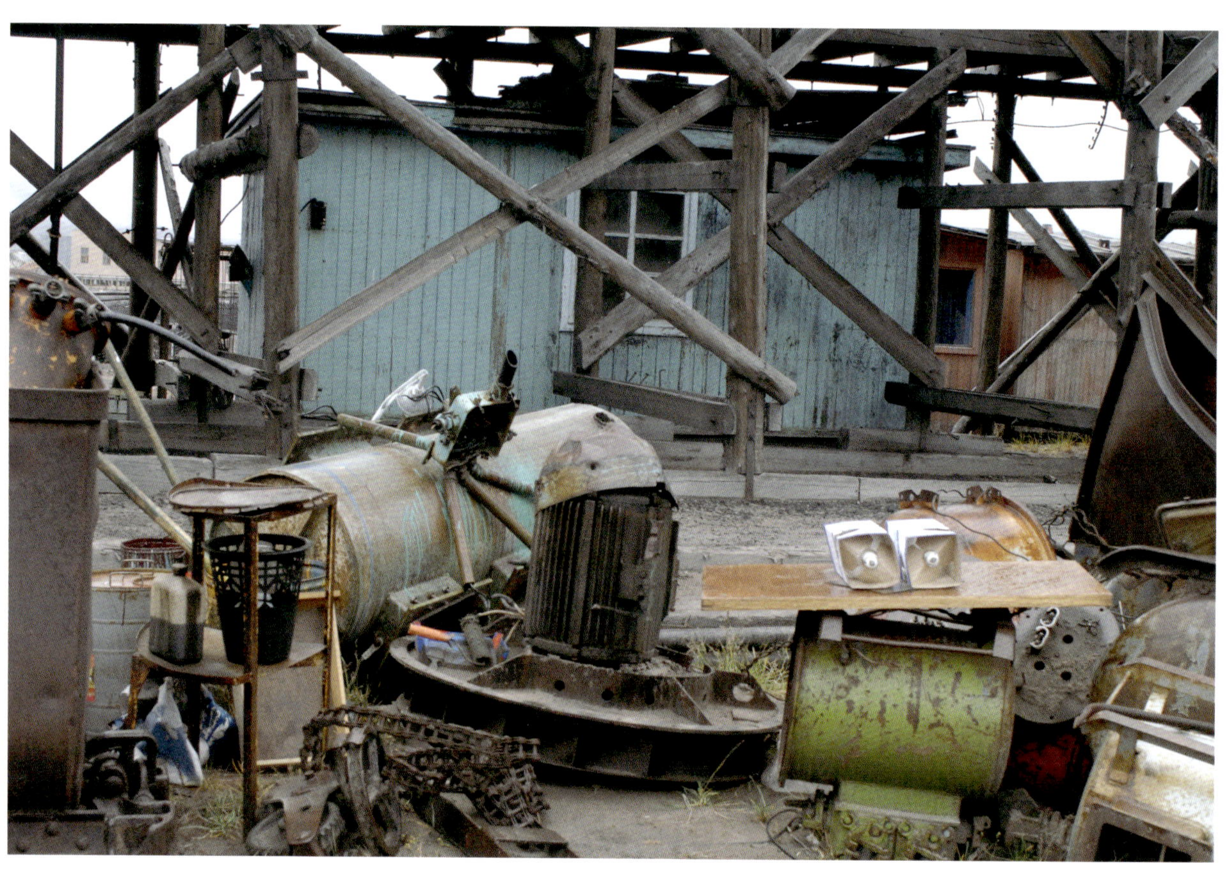

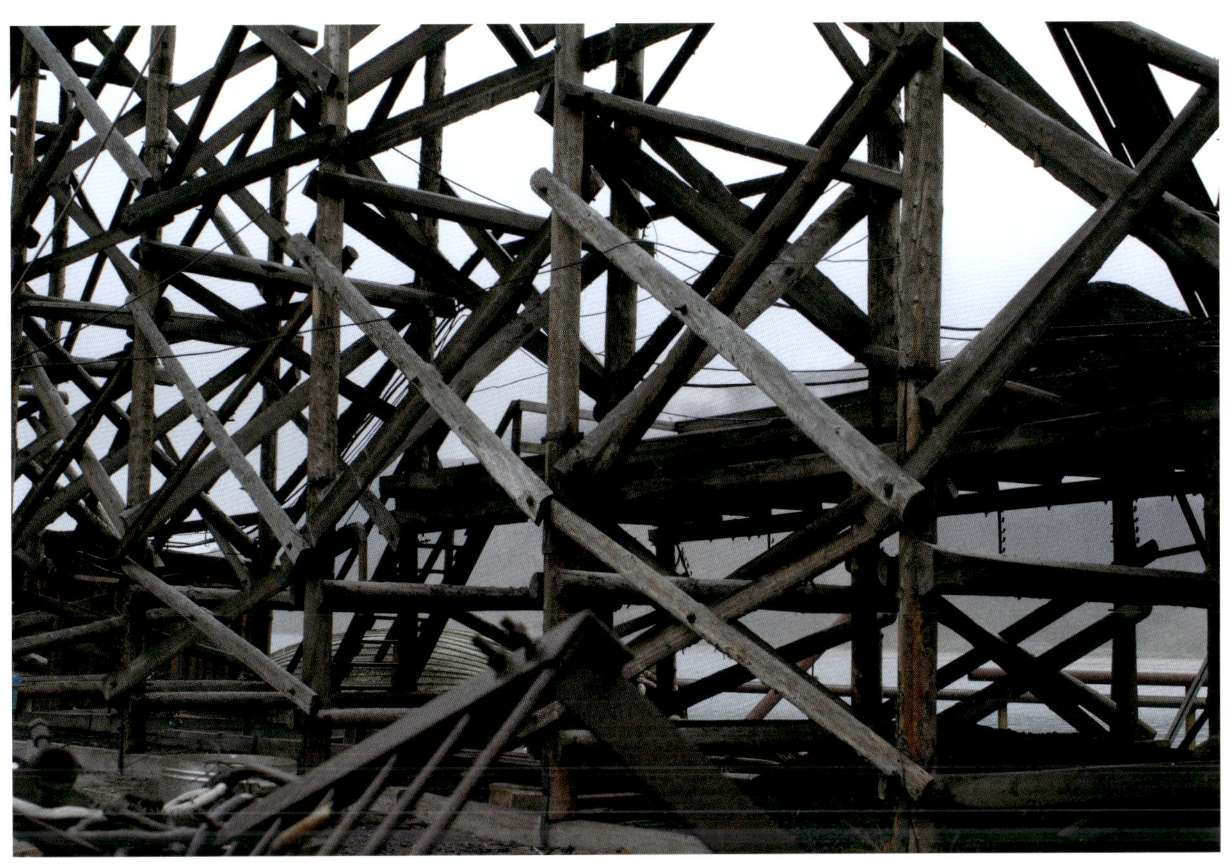

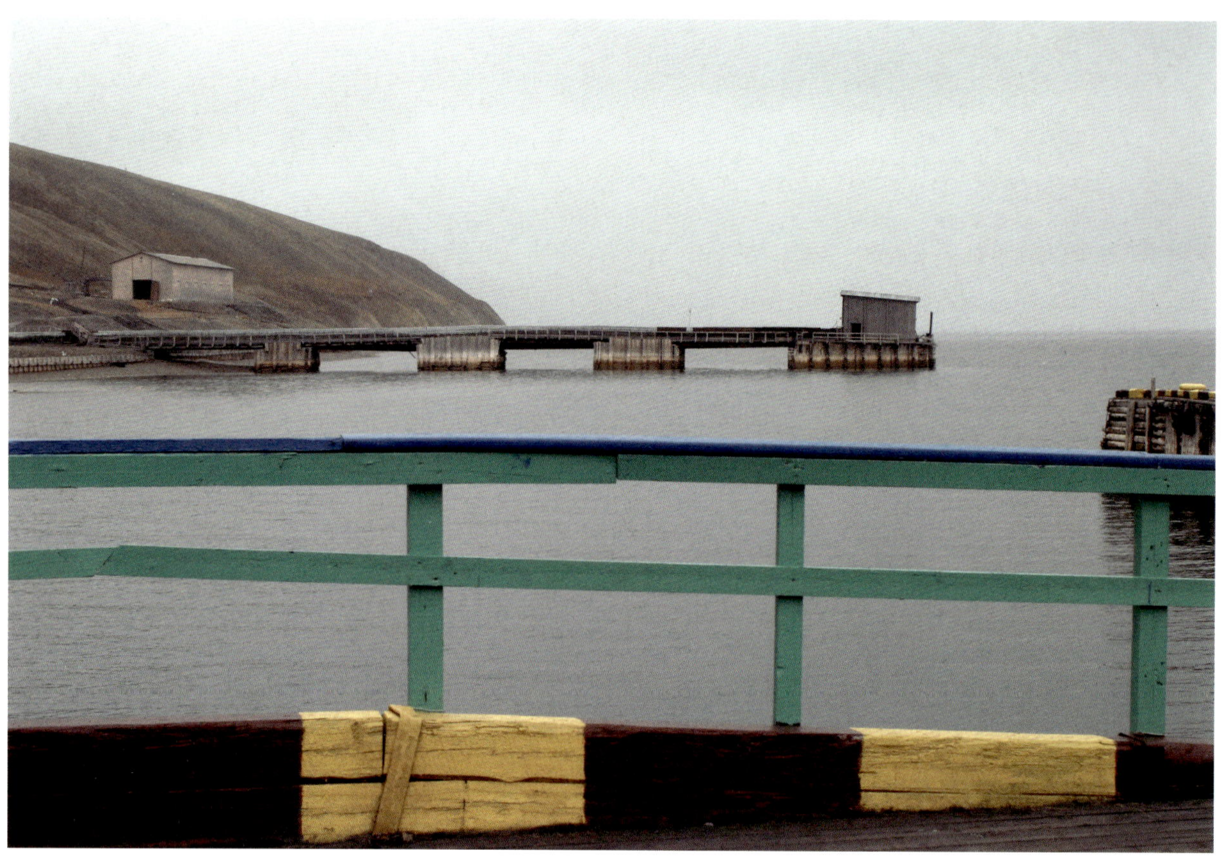

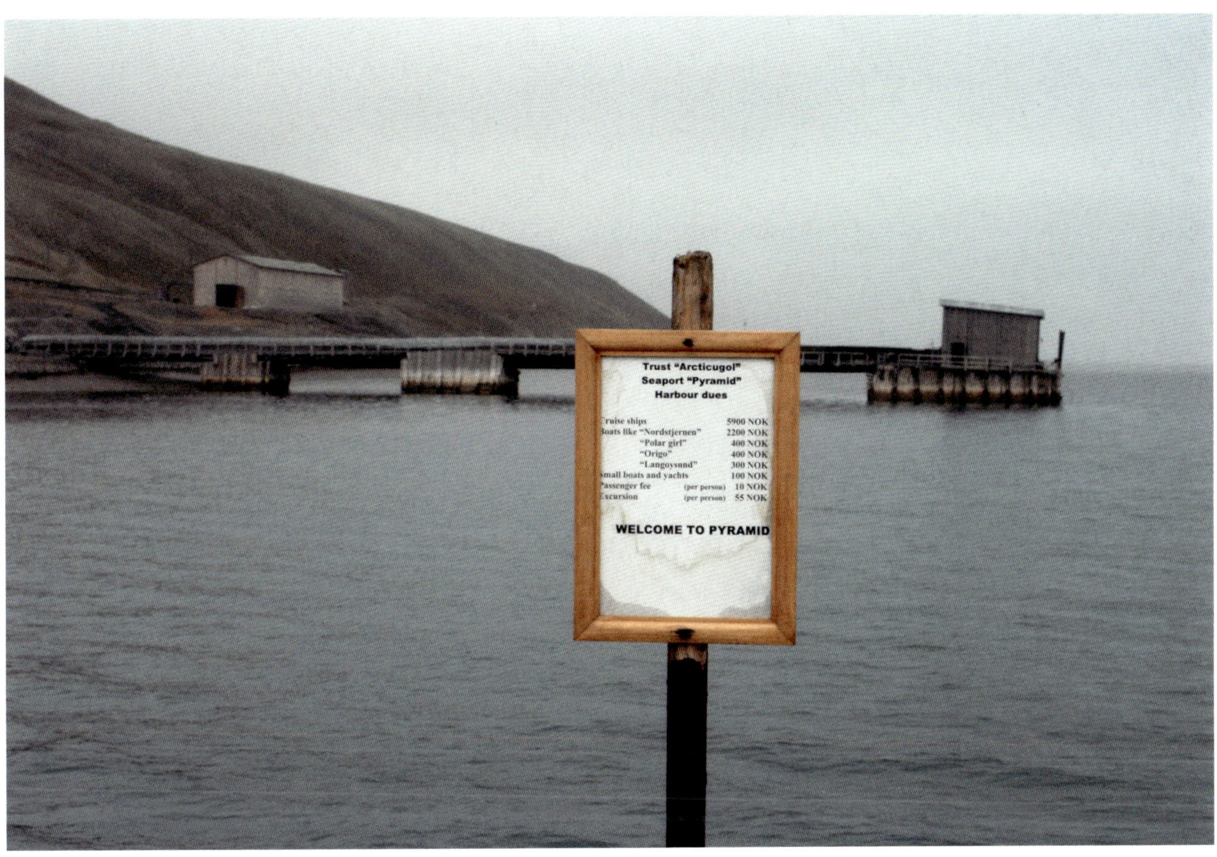
Trust “Arcticugol”
Seaport “Pyramid”
Harbour dues
ruise ships 5900 NOK
oats like “Nordstjernen” 2200 NOK
“Polar girl” 400 NOK
“Origo” 400 NOK
“Langoysund” 300 NOK
mall boats and yachts 100 NOK
assenger fee (per person) 10 NOK
xcursion (per person) 55 NOK
WELCOME TO PYRAMID

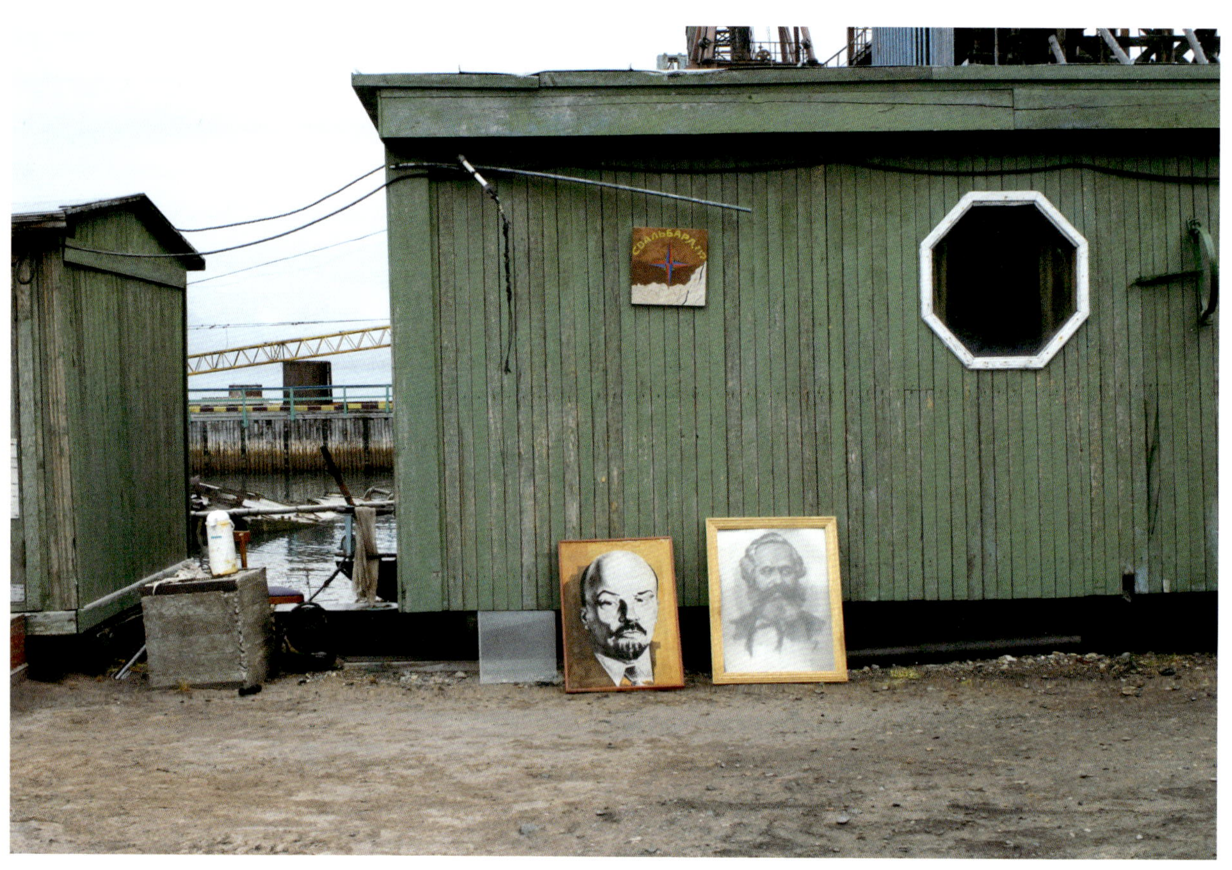

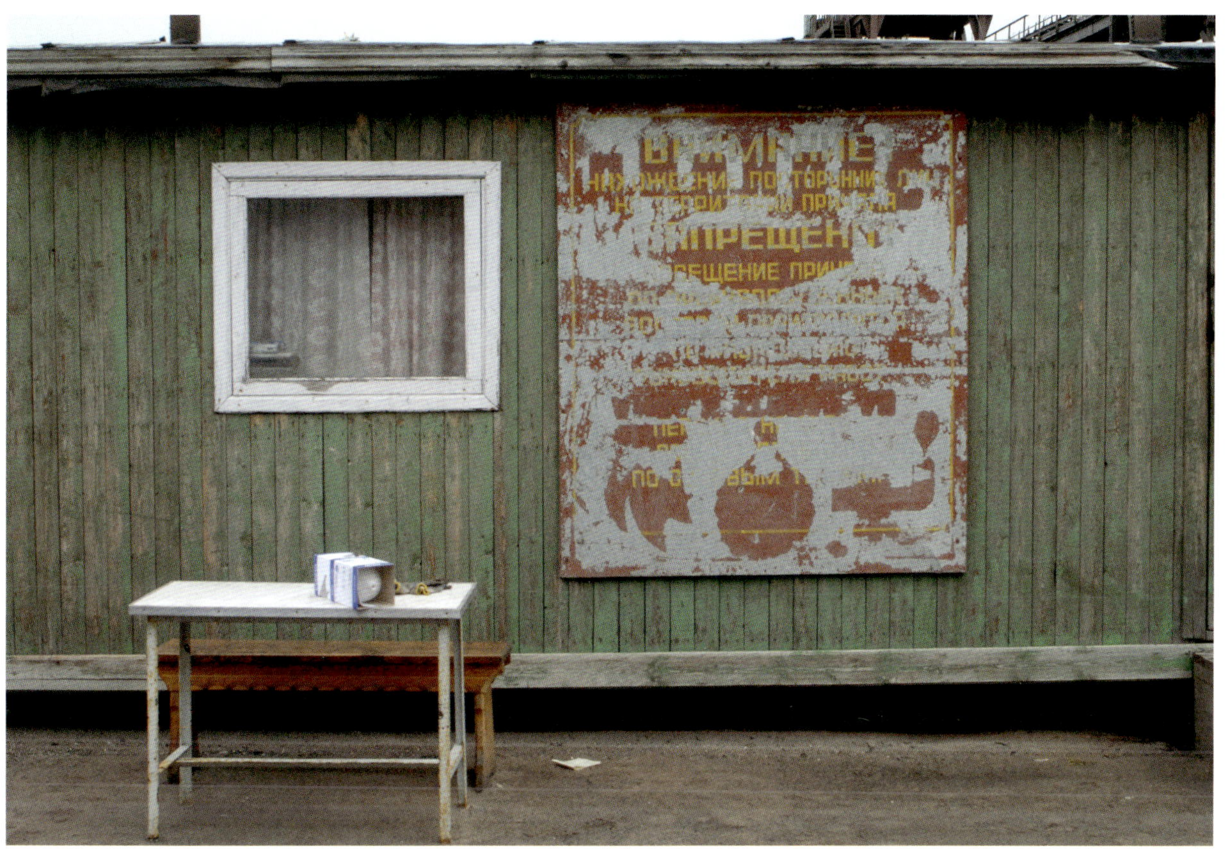

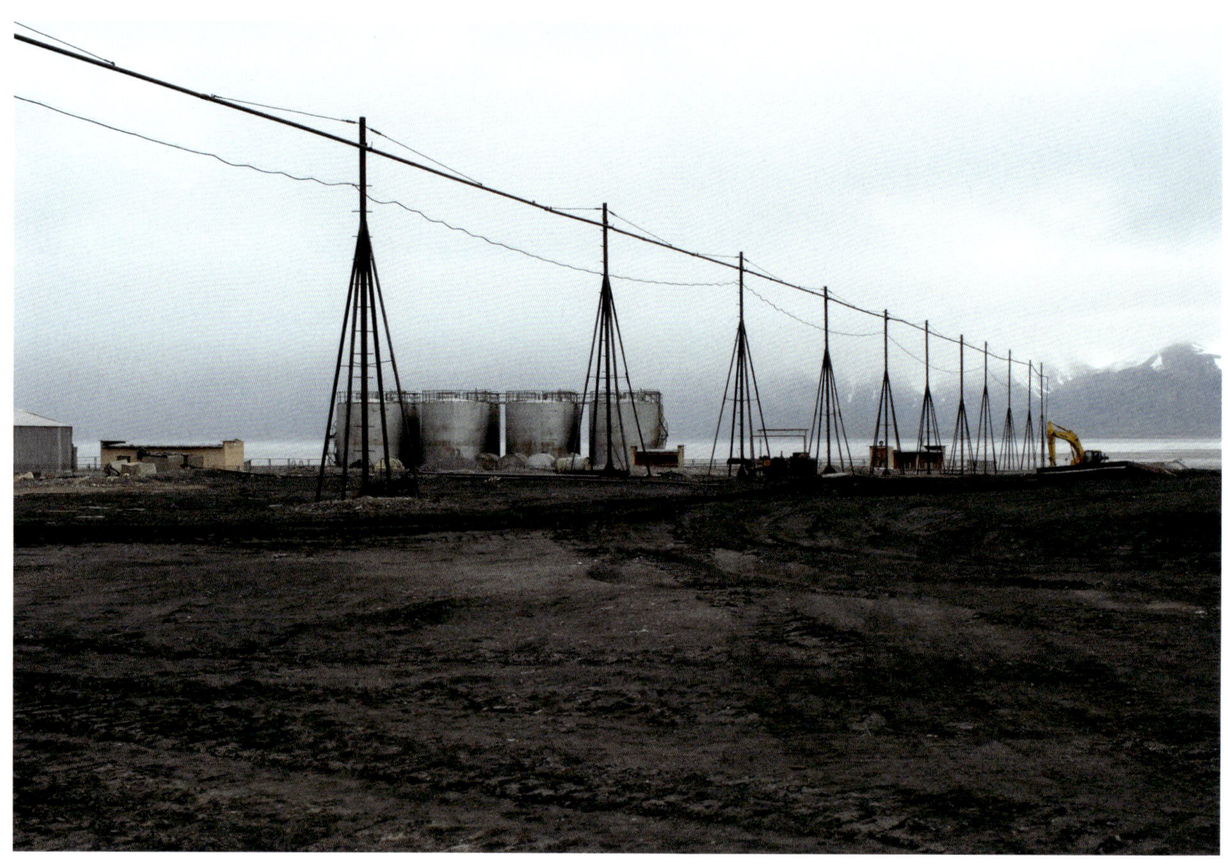

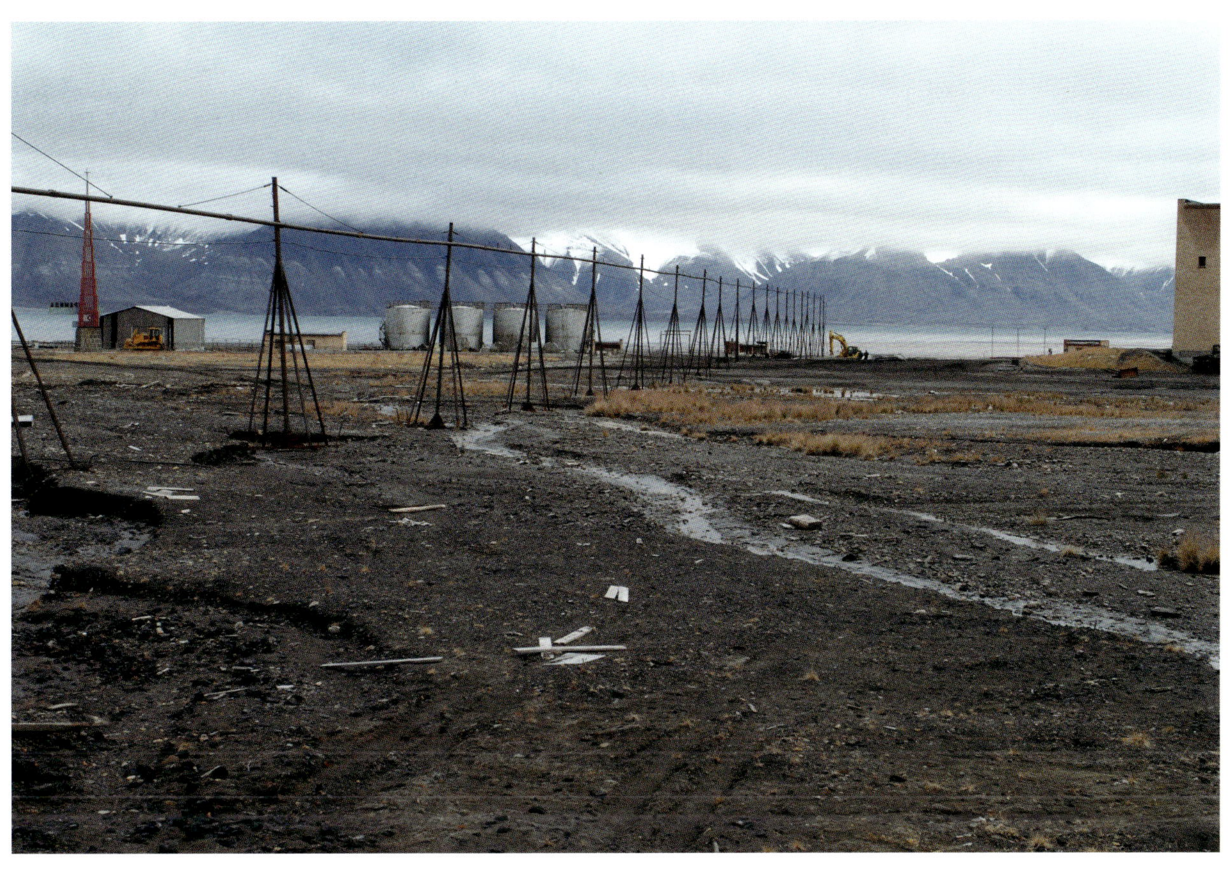

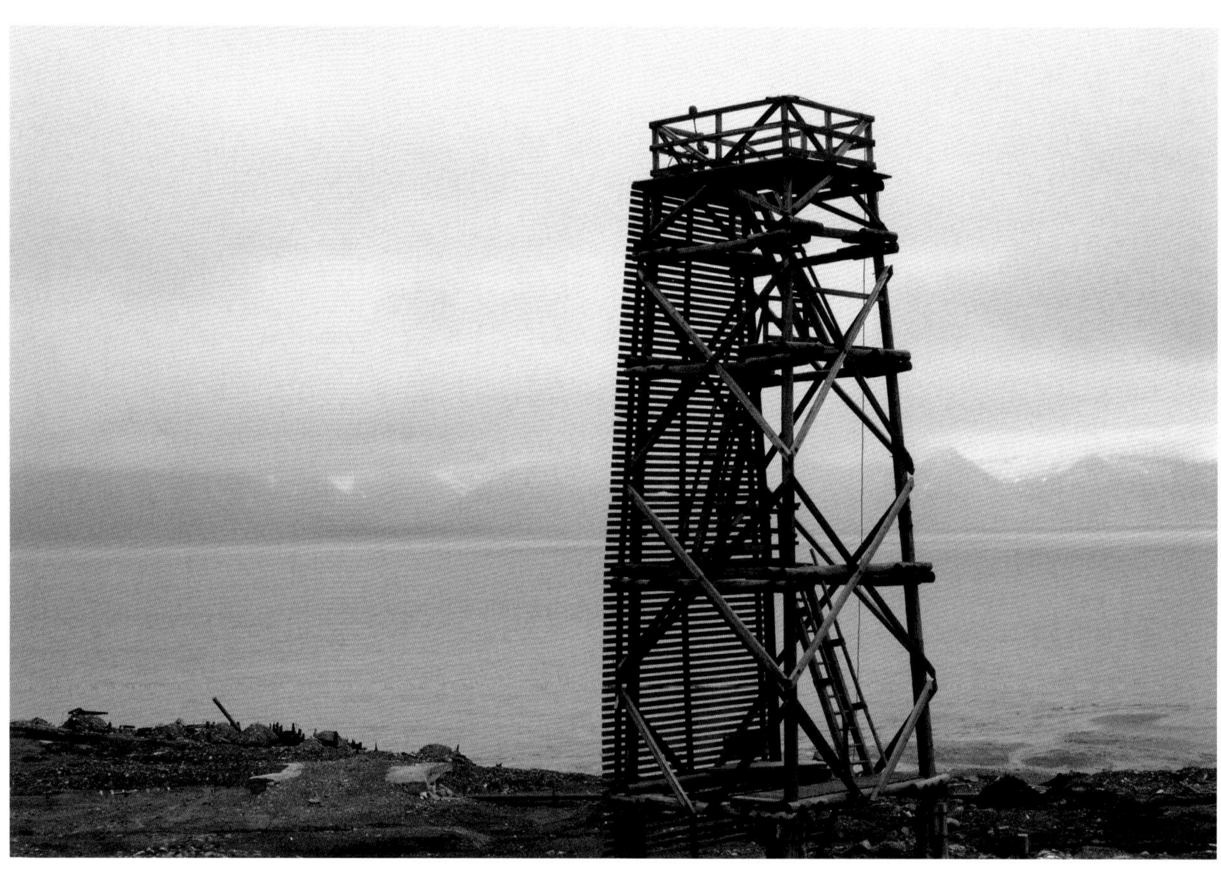

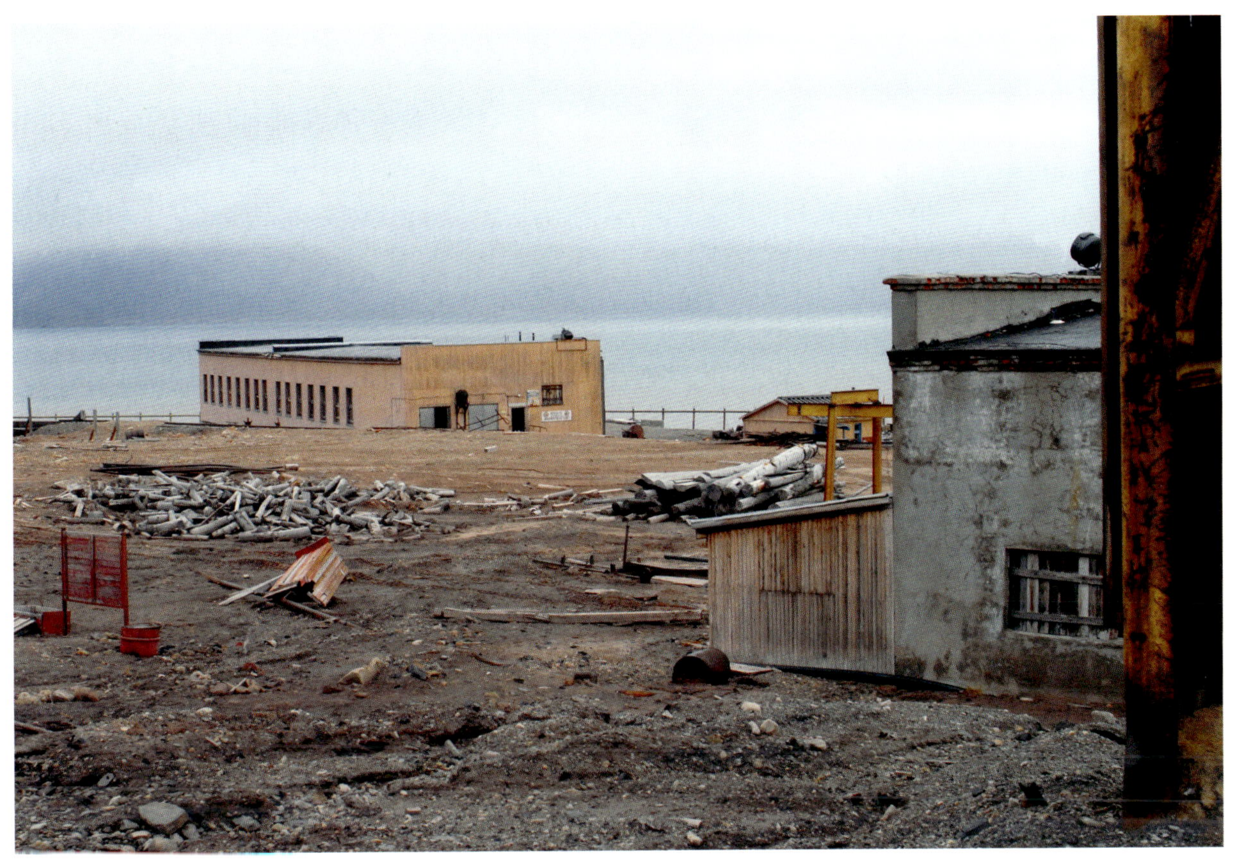

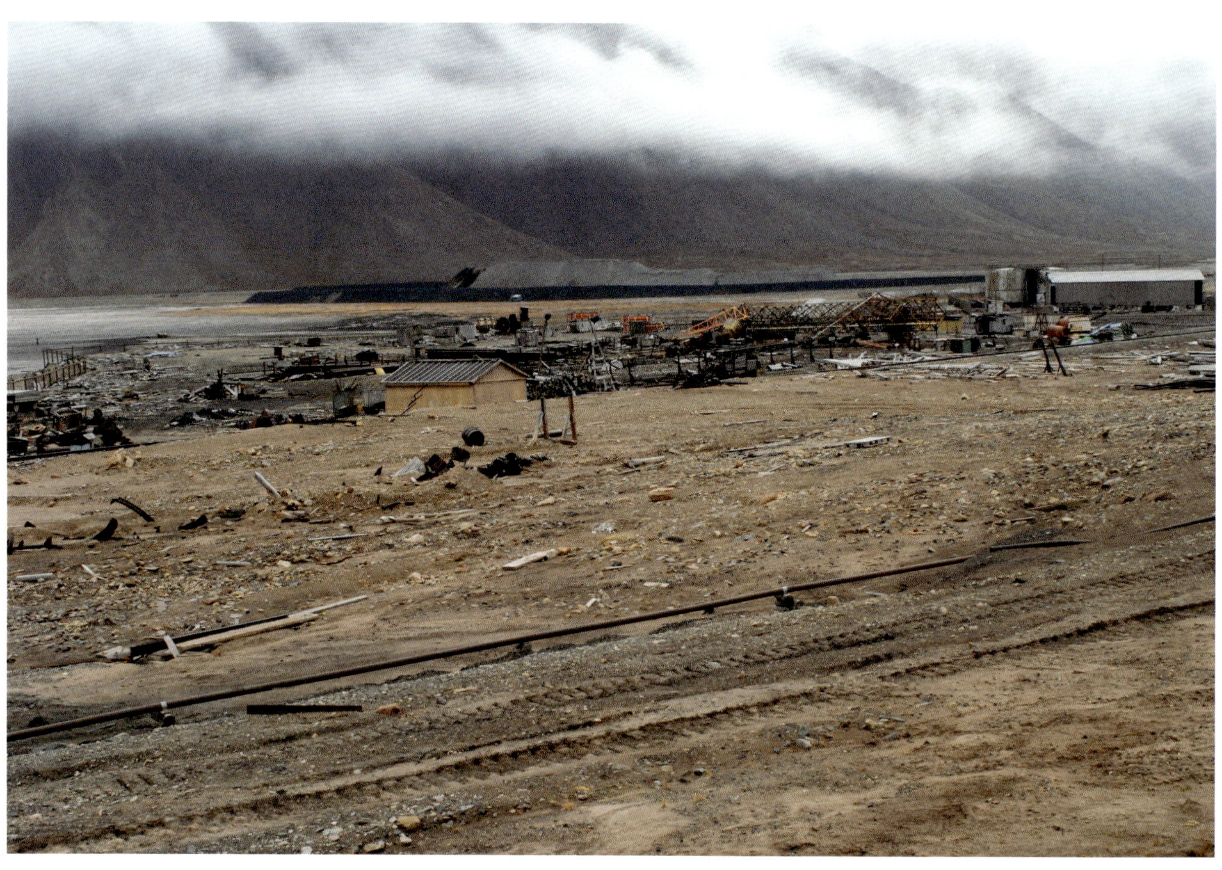

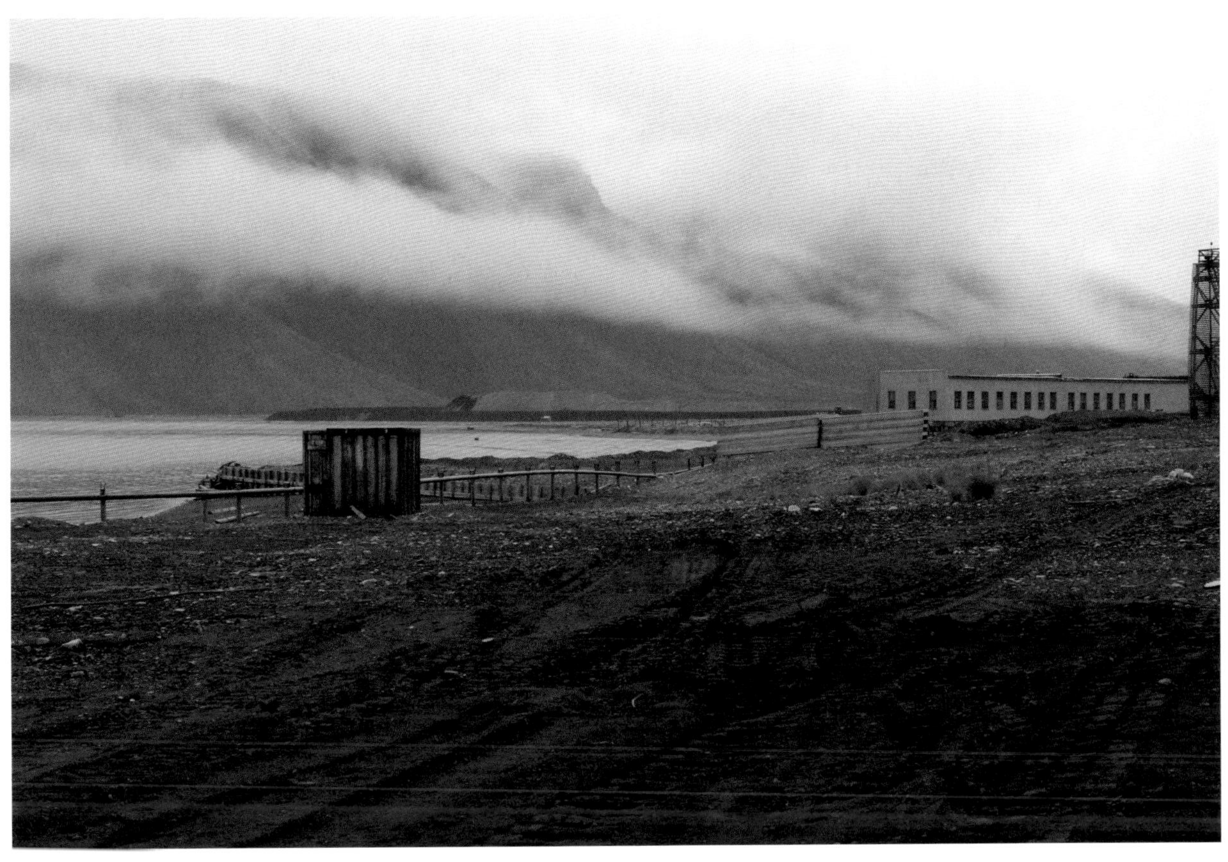

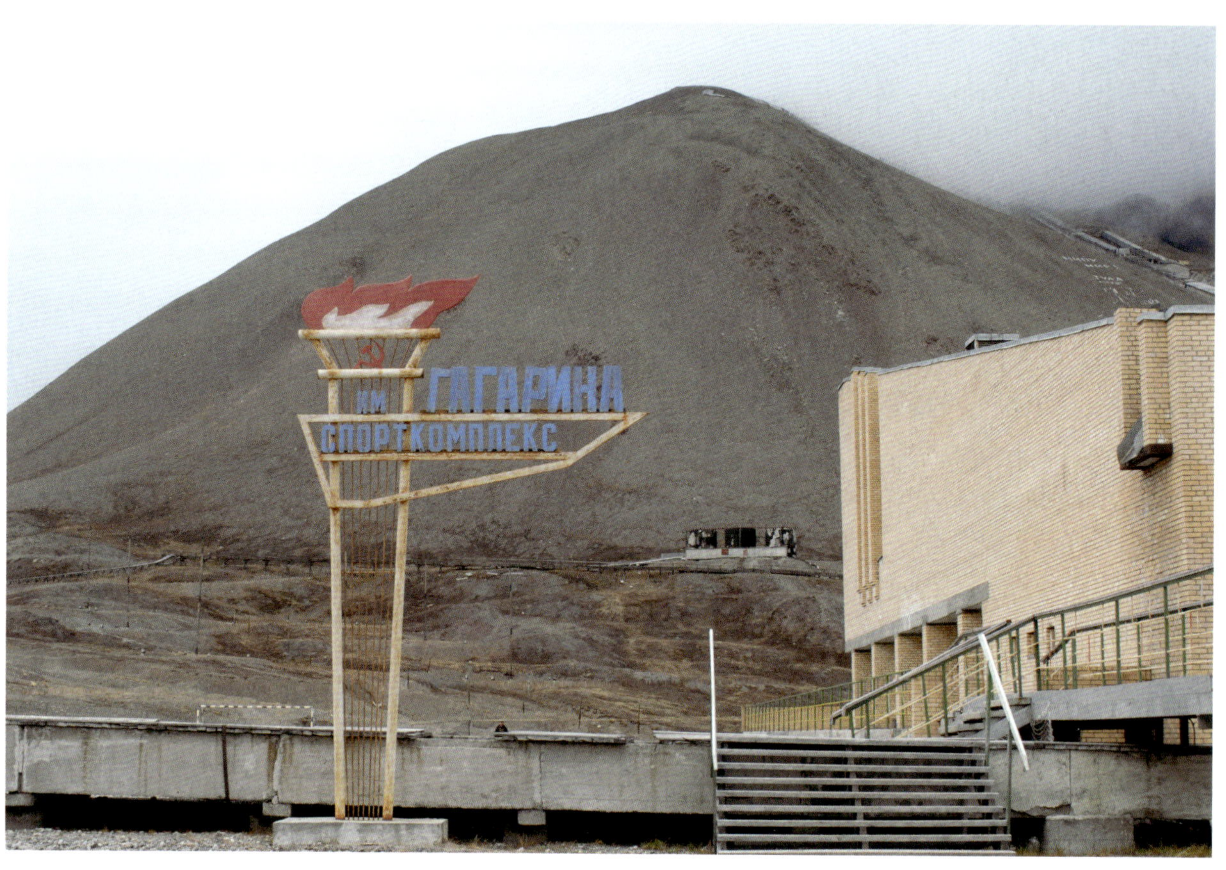
ИМ ГАГАРИНА
СПОРТКОМПЛЕКС

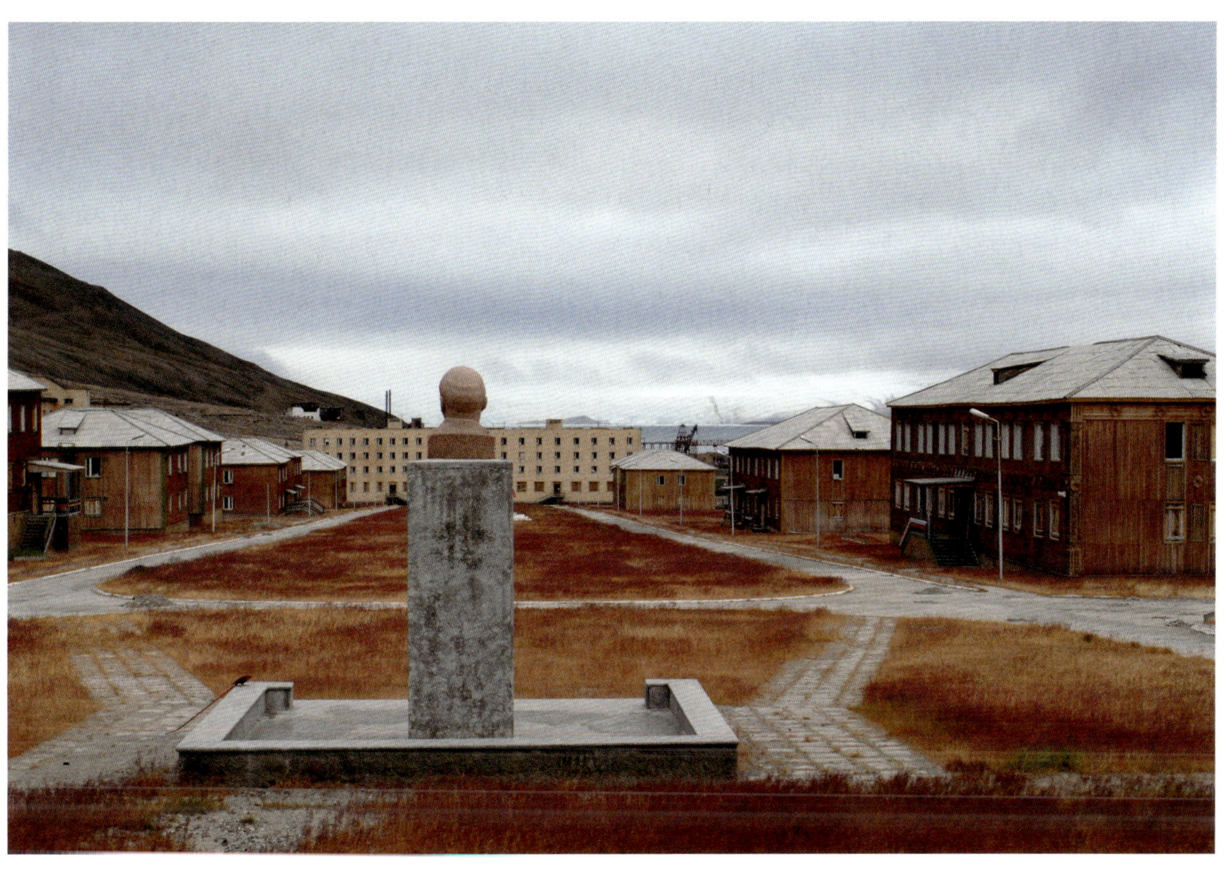

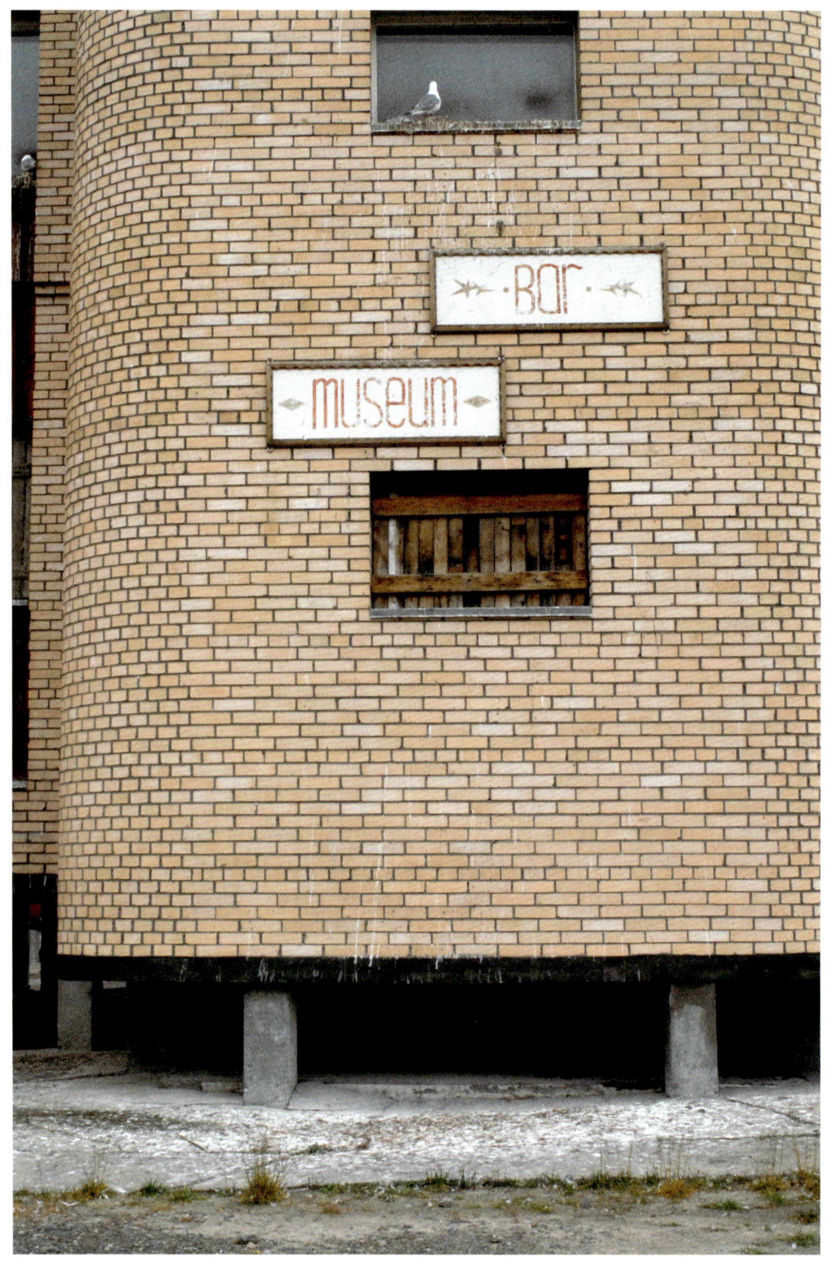
Bar
museum

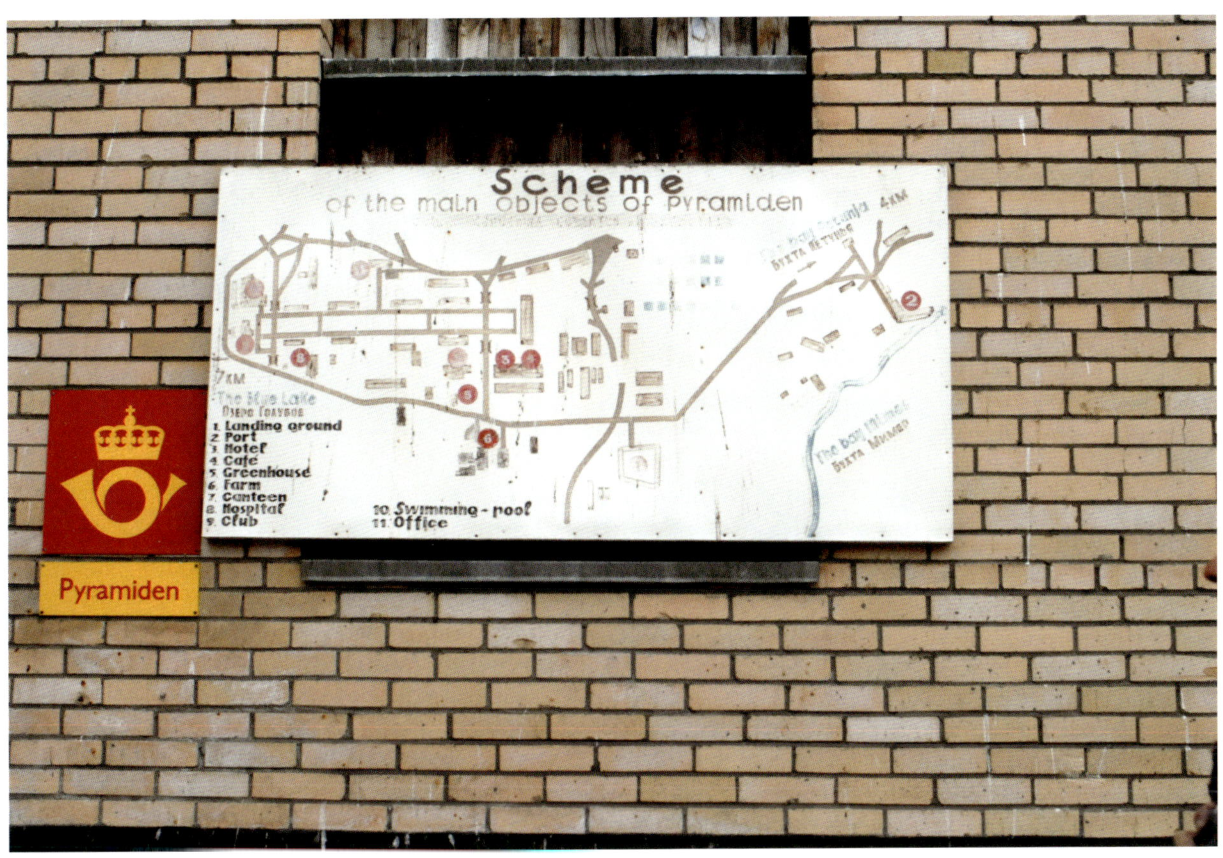
Scheme
of the main objects of Pyramiden
4KM
7KM
1. Landing ground
2. Port
3. Hotel
4. Cafe
5. Greenhouse
6. Farm
7. Canteen
8. Hospital
9. Club
10. Swimming - pool
11. Office
Pyramiden

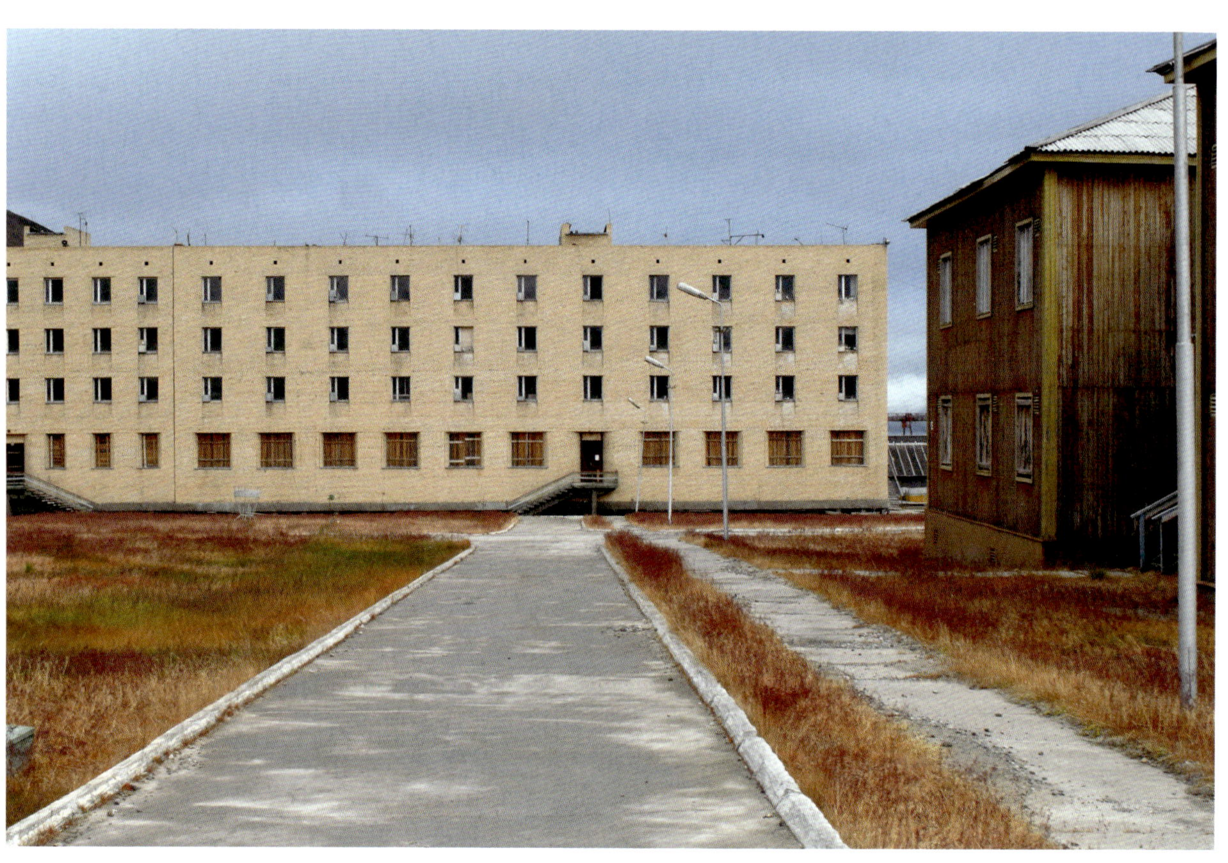

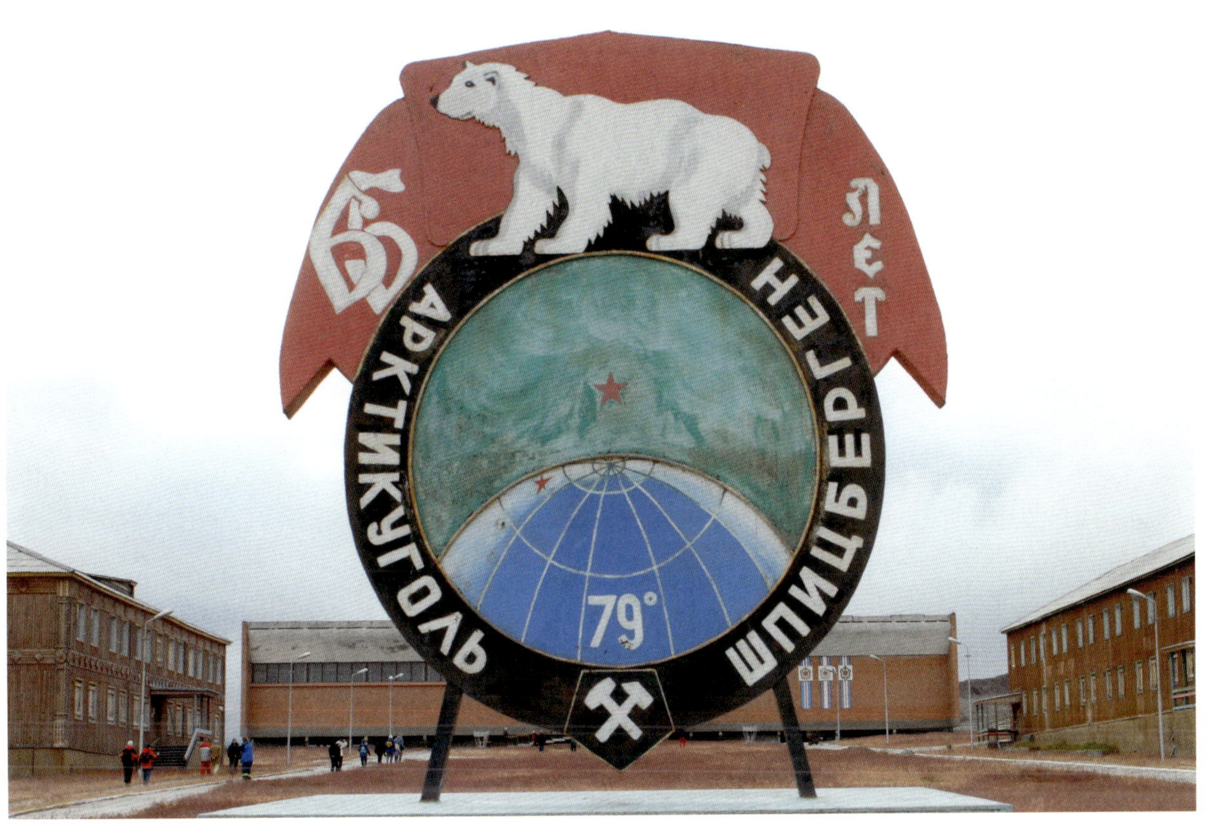
60 ЛЕТ
АРКТИКУГОЛЬ
ШПИЦБЕРГЕН
79°

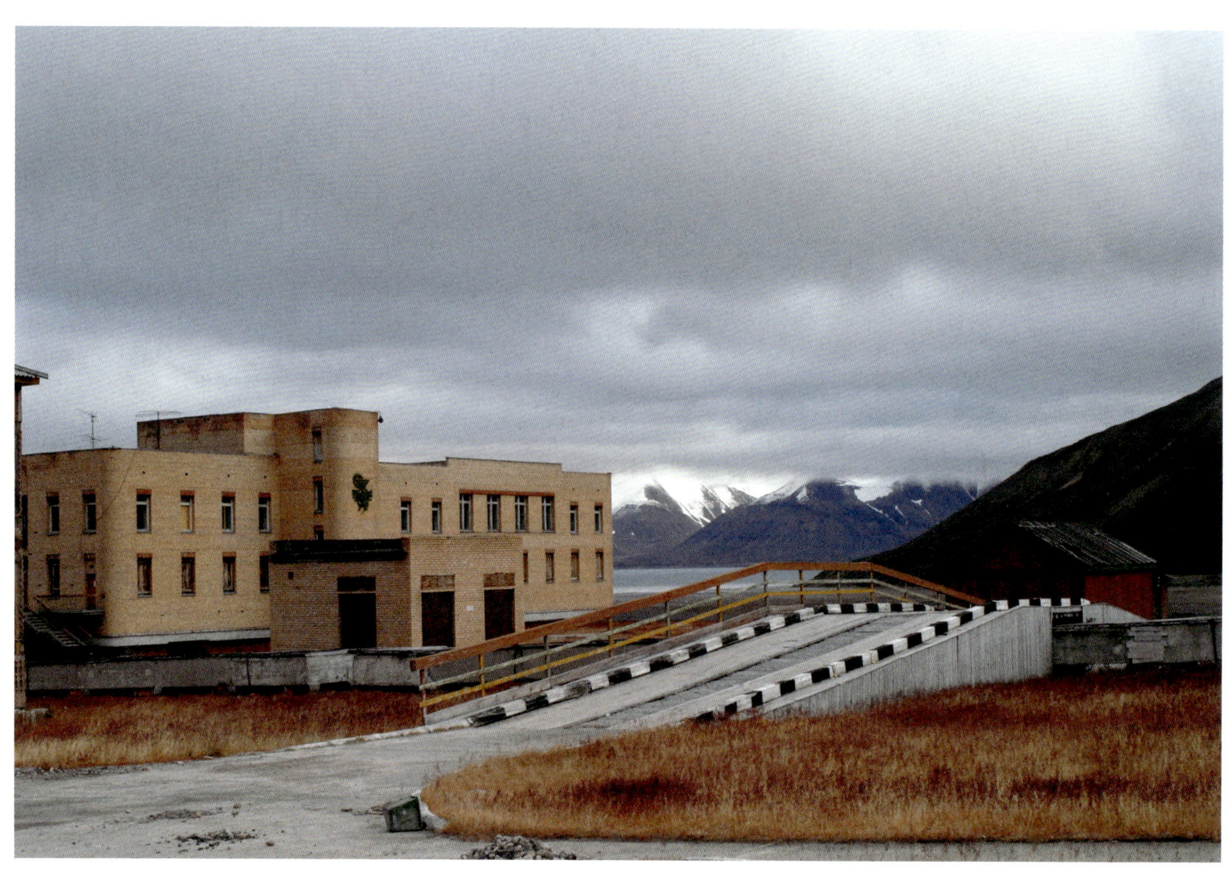

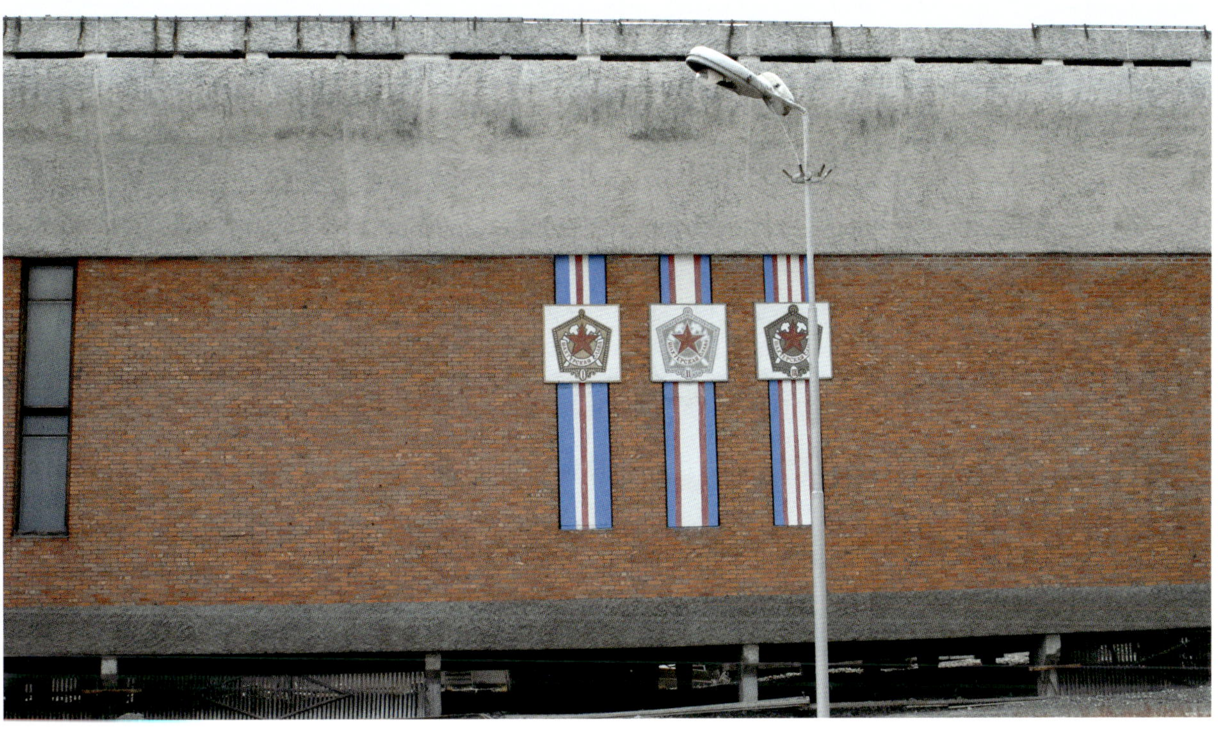

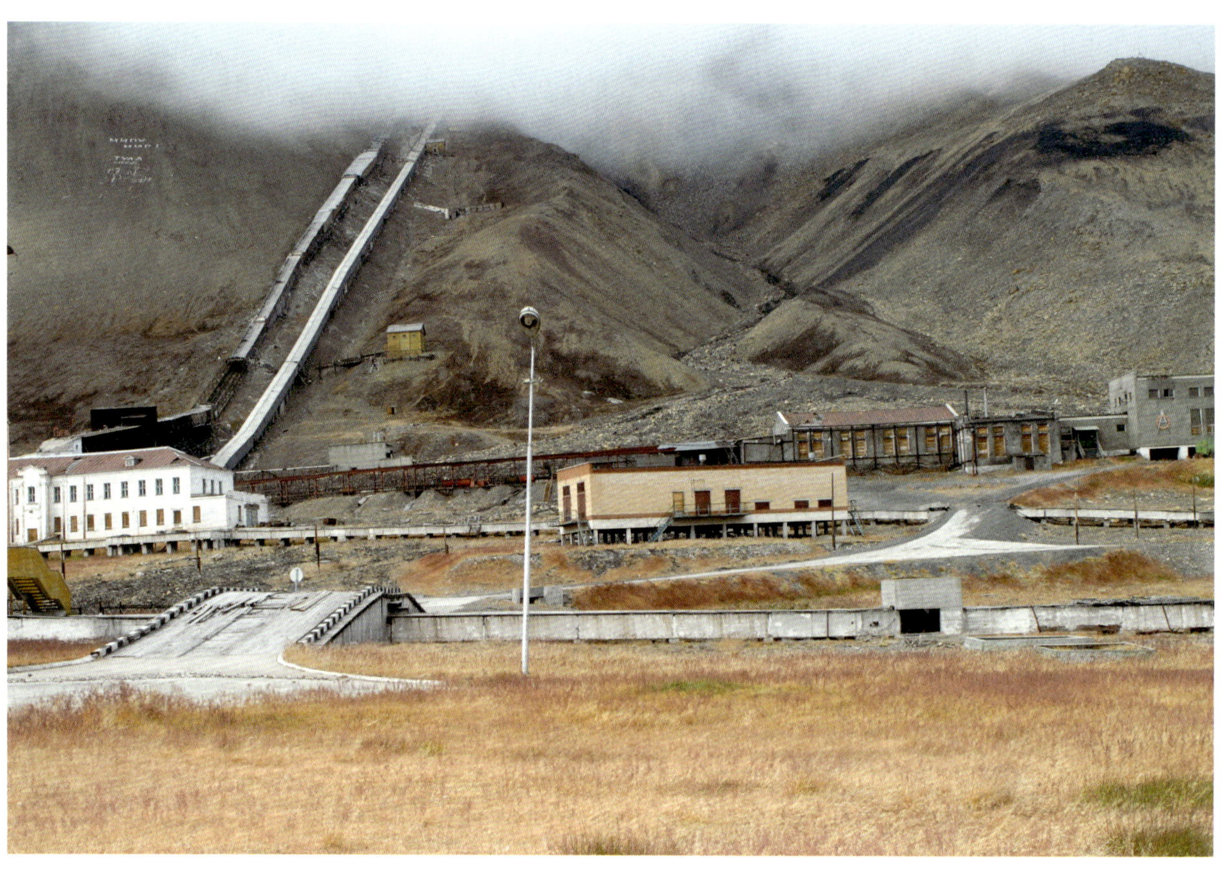

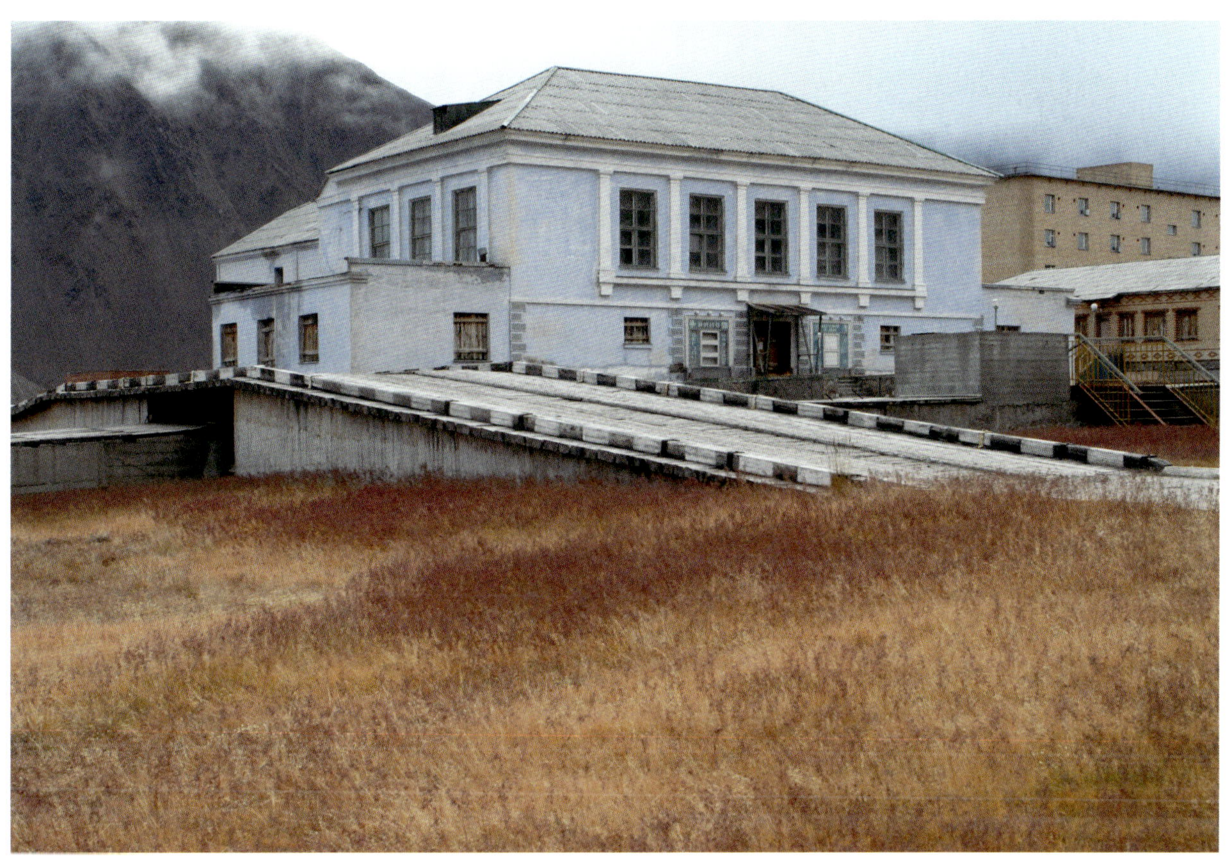

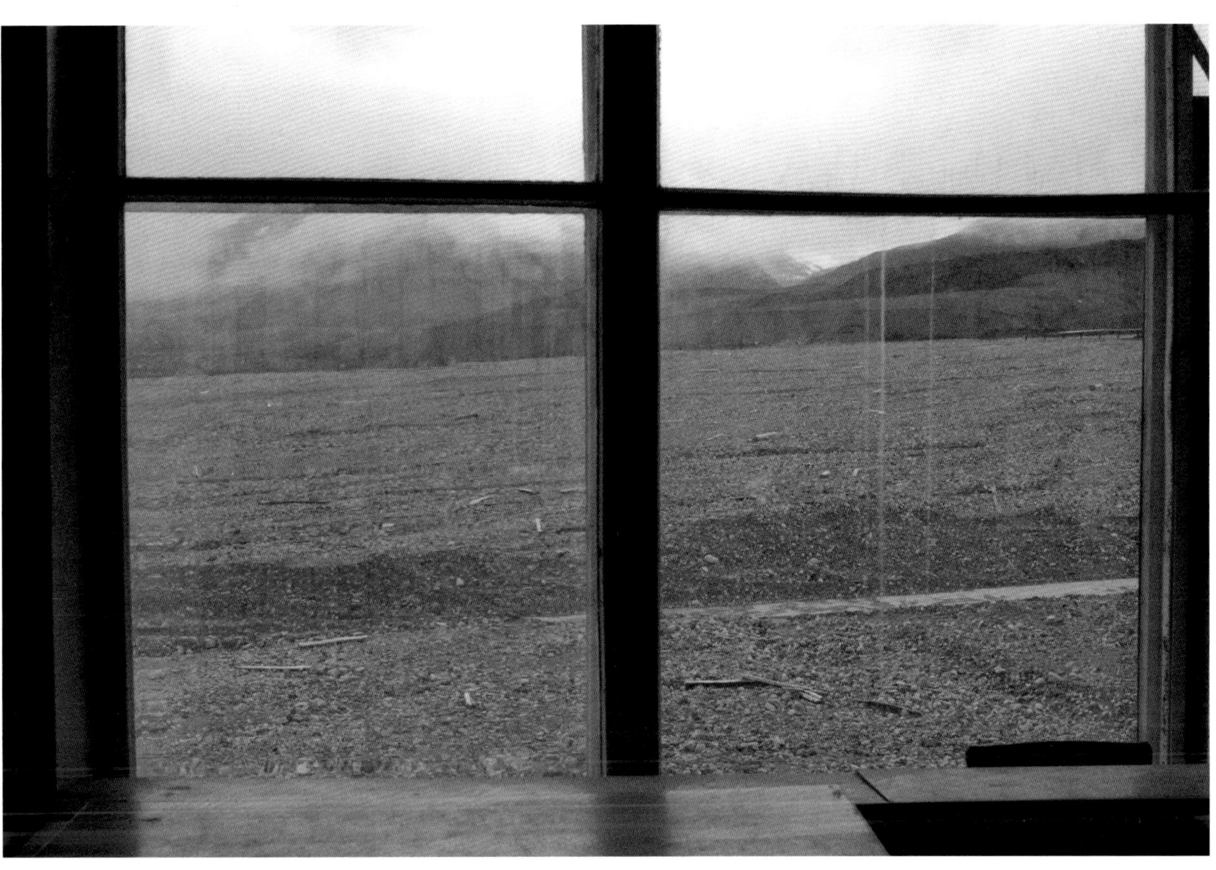

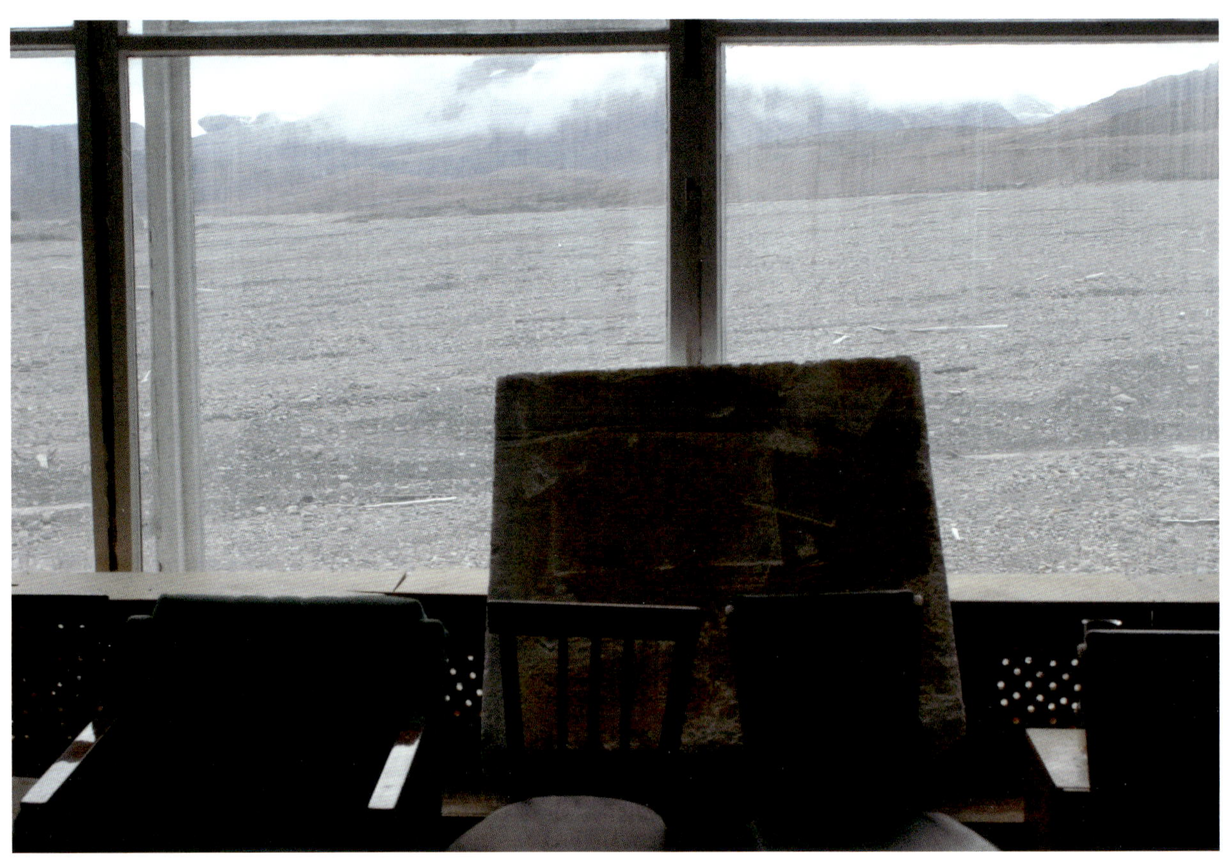

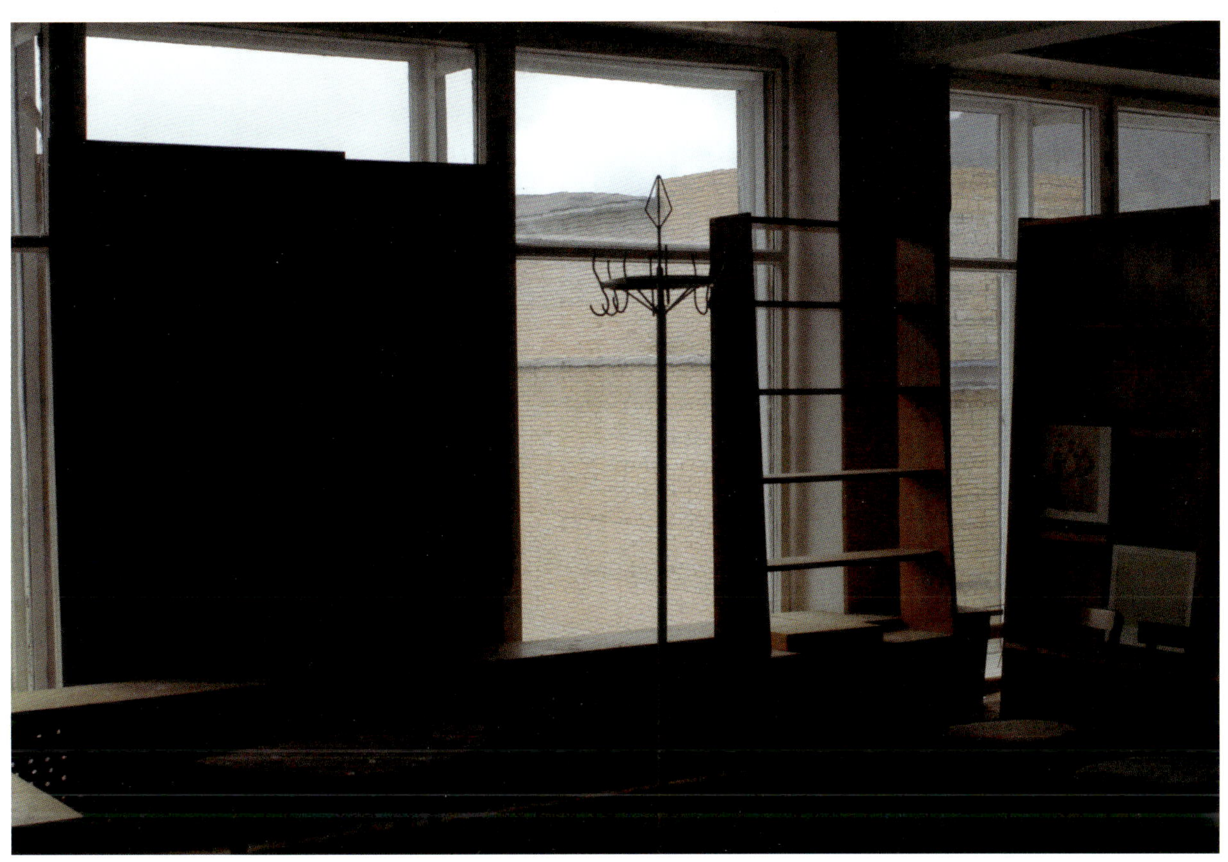

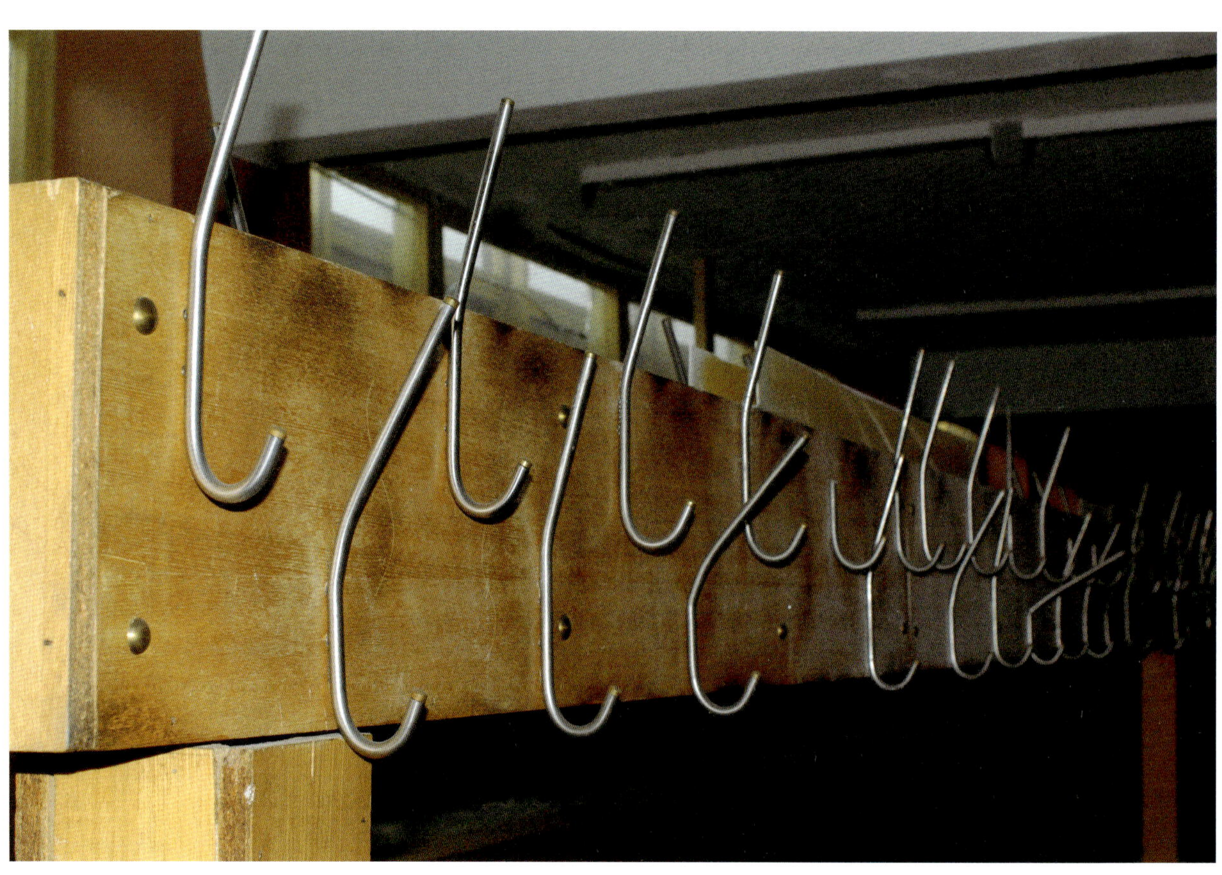

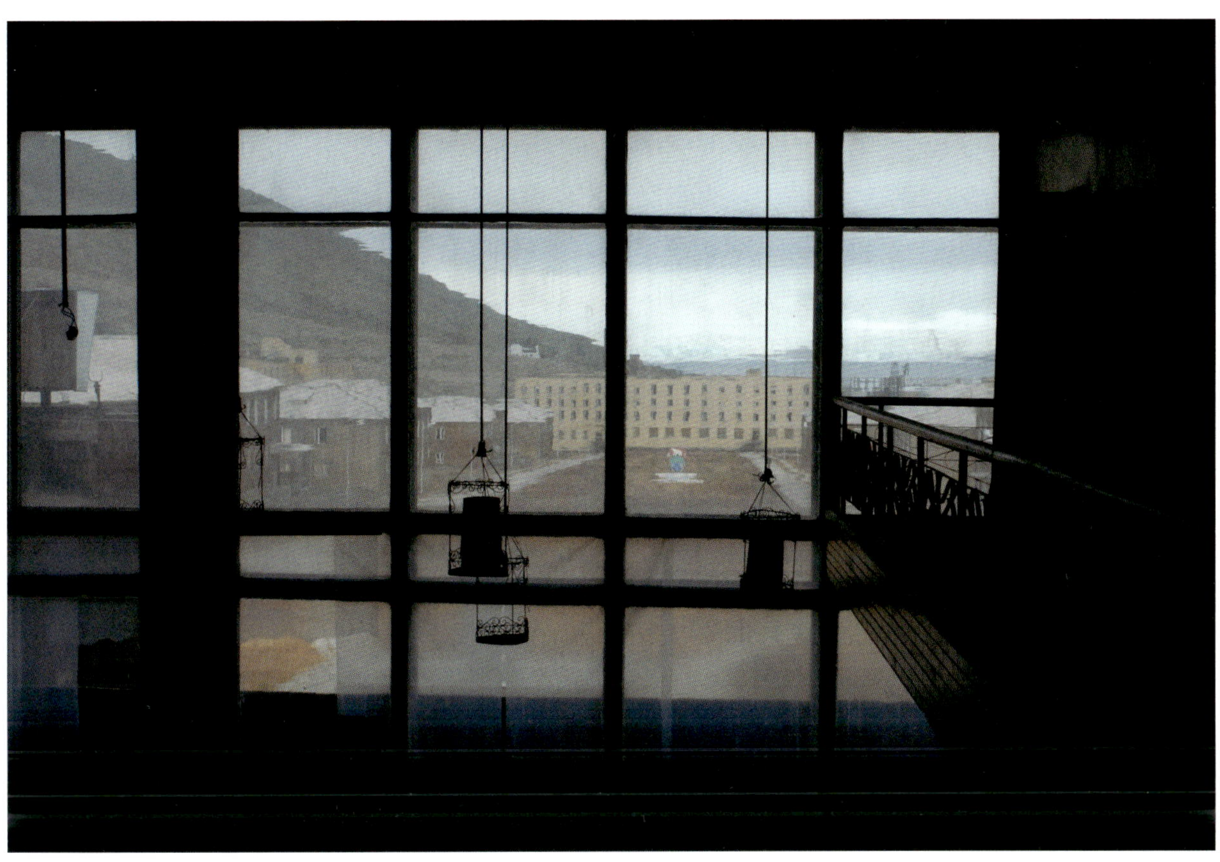

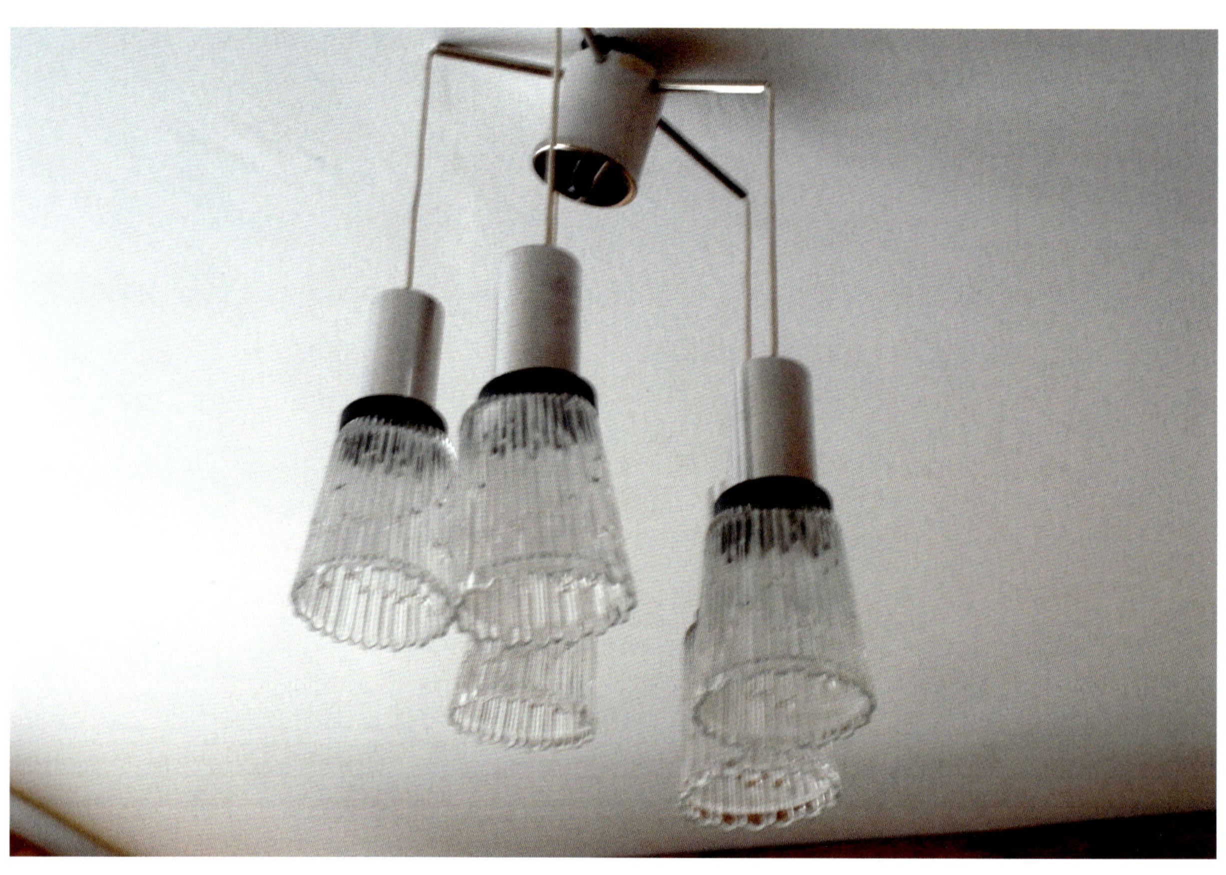

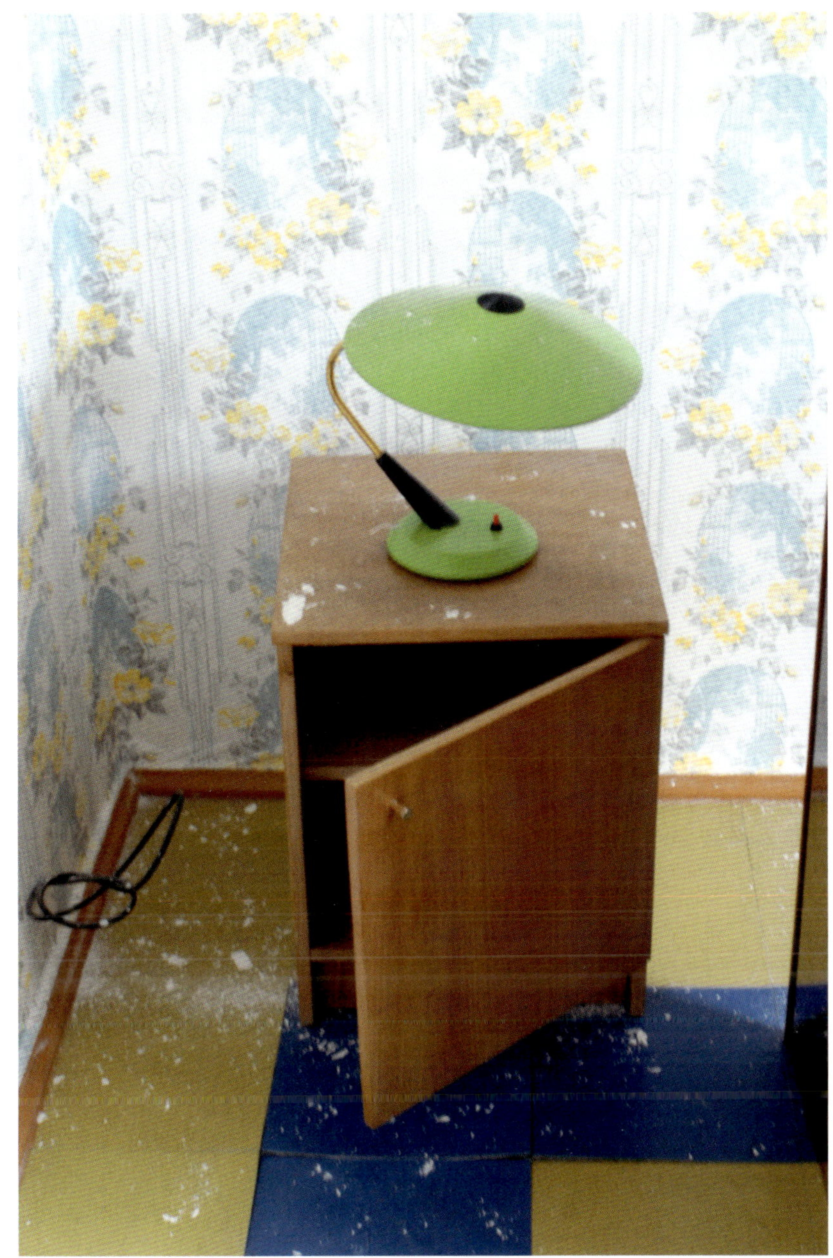

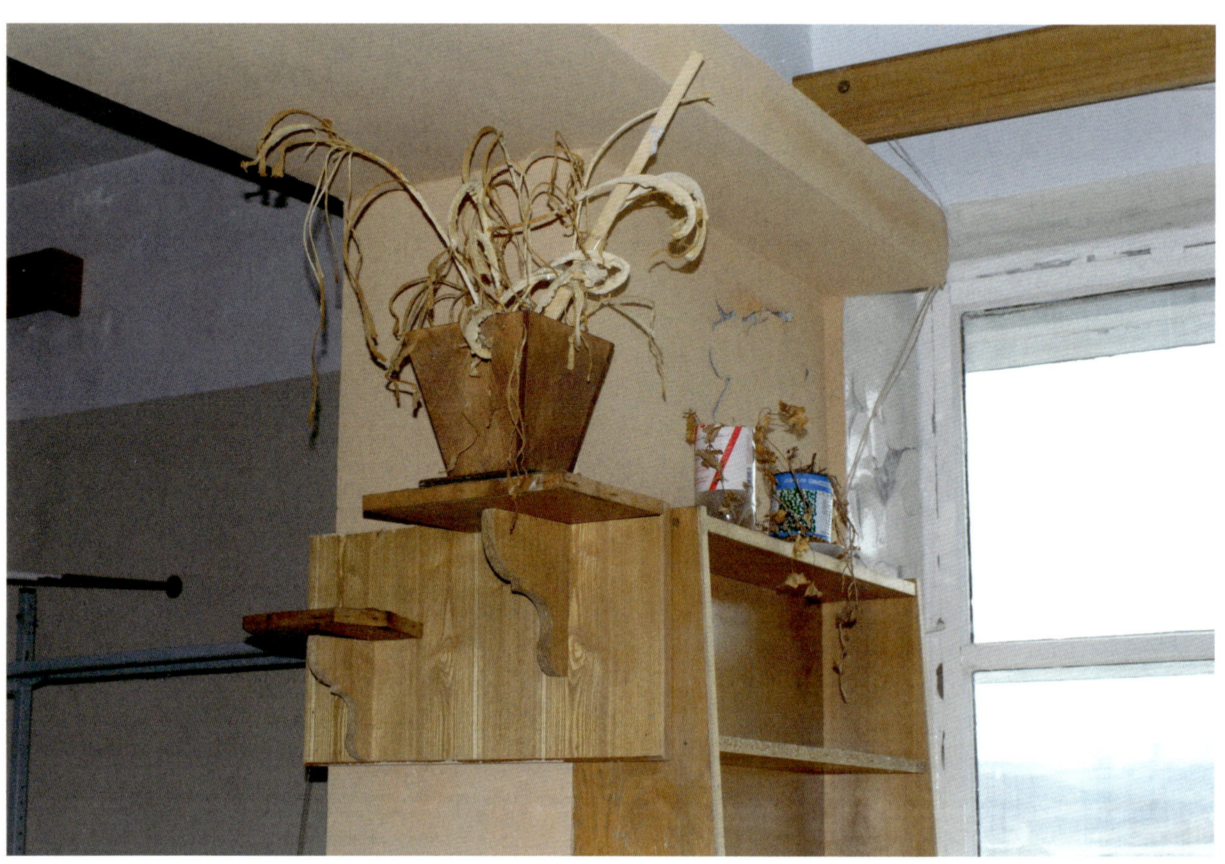

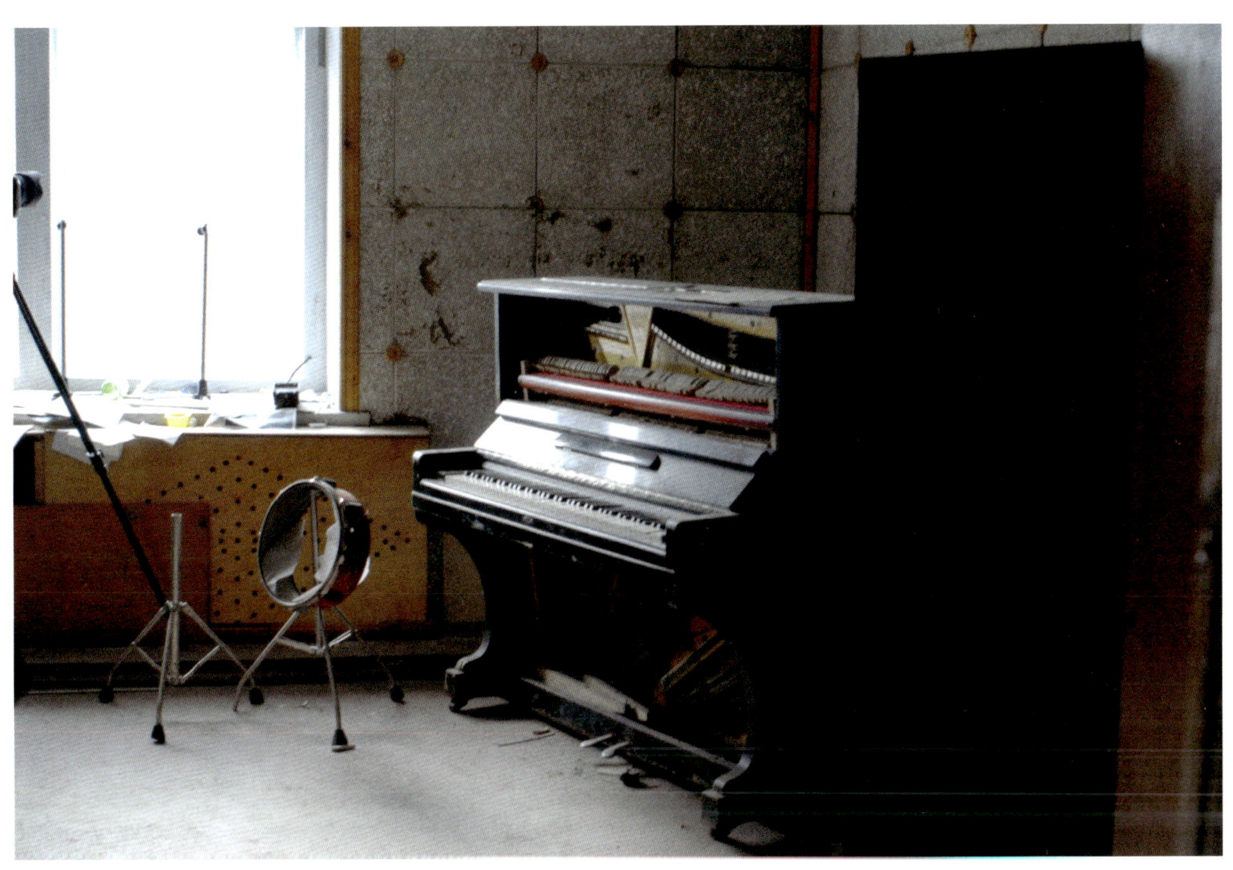

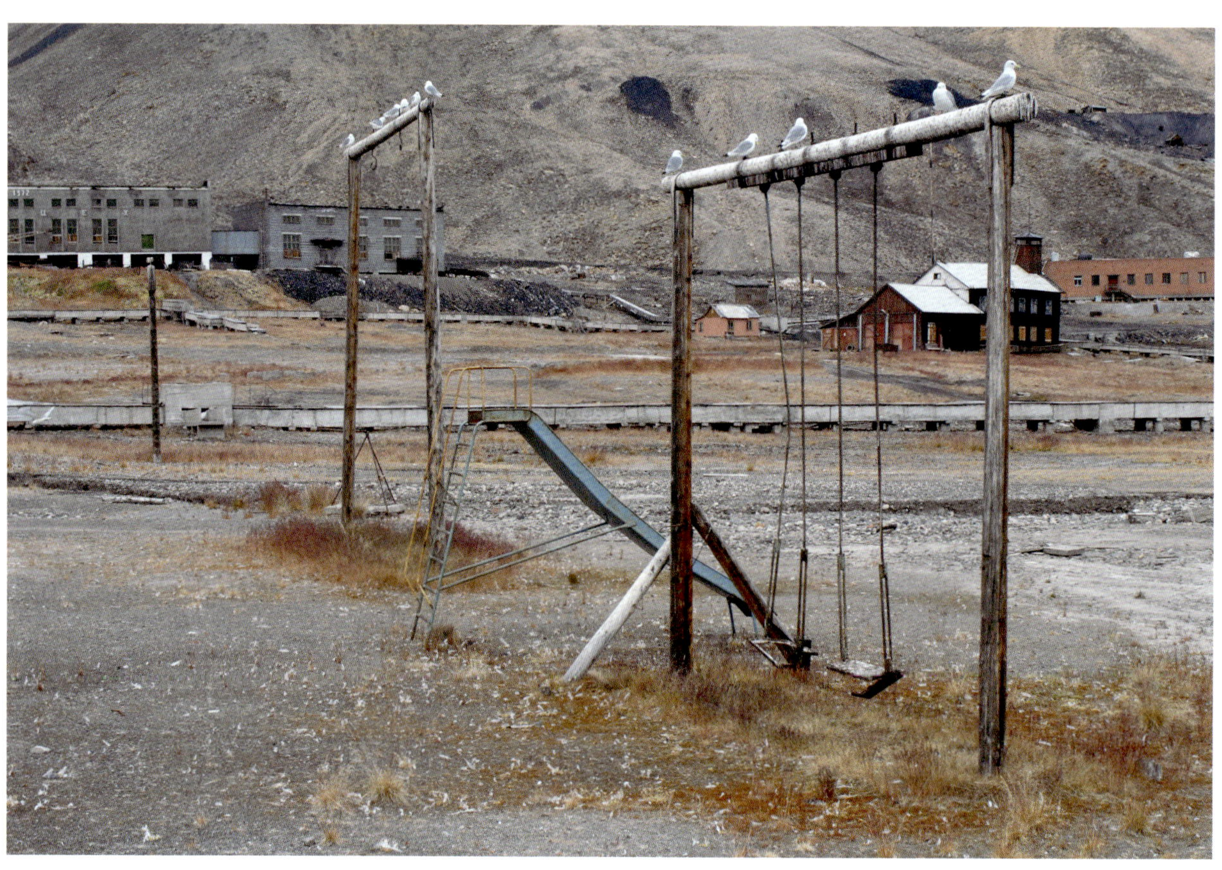

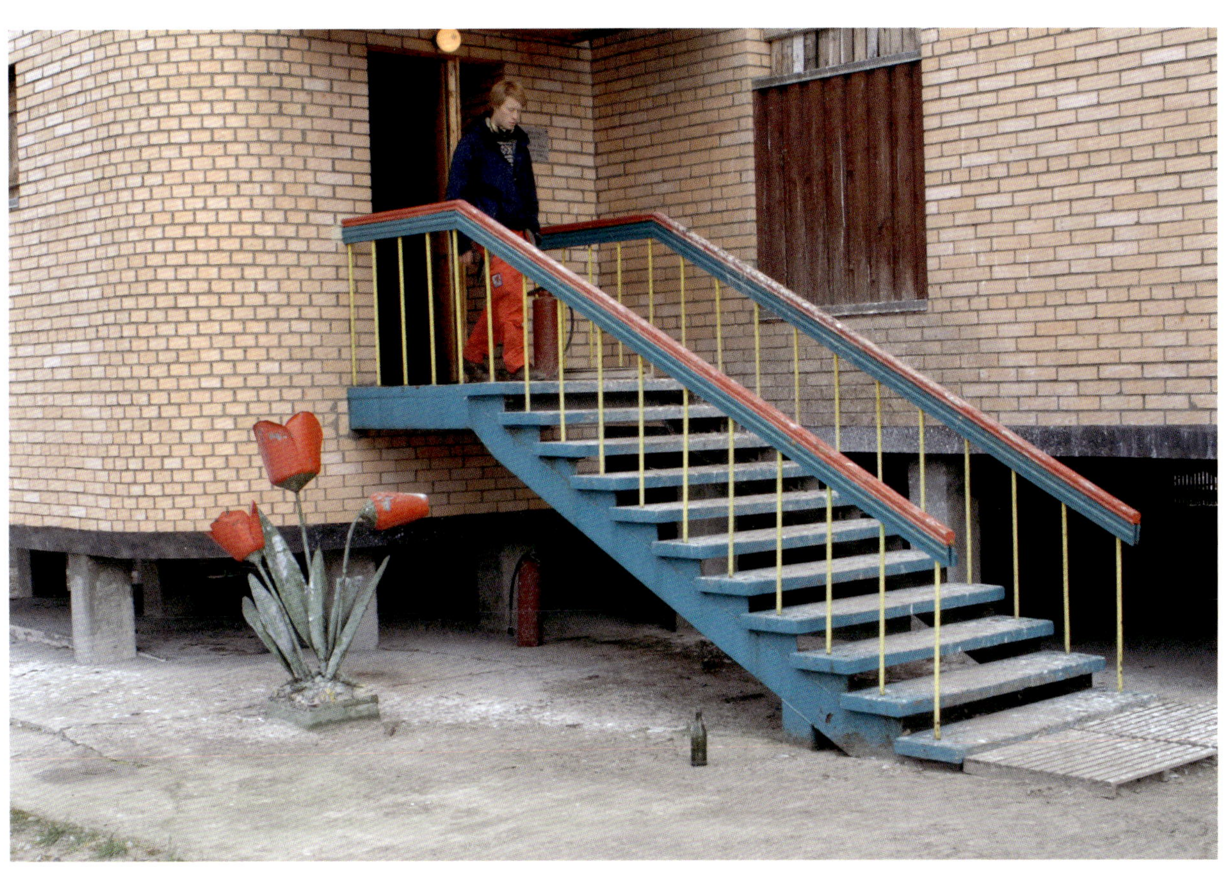

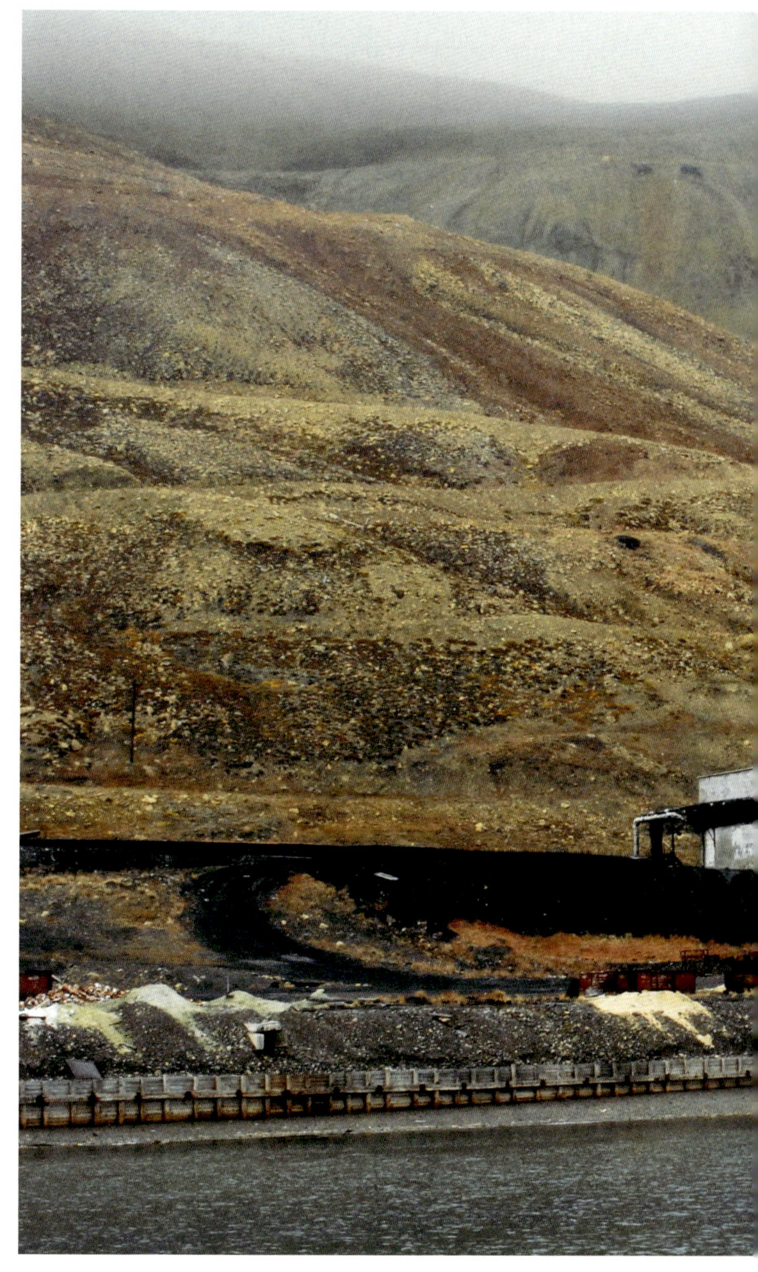

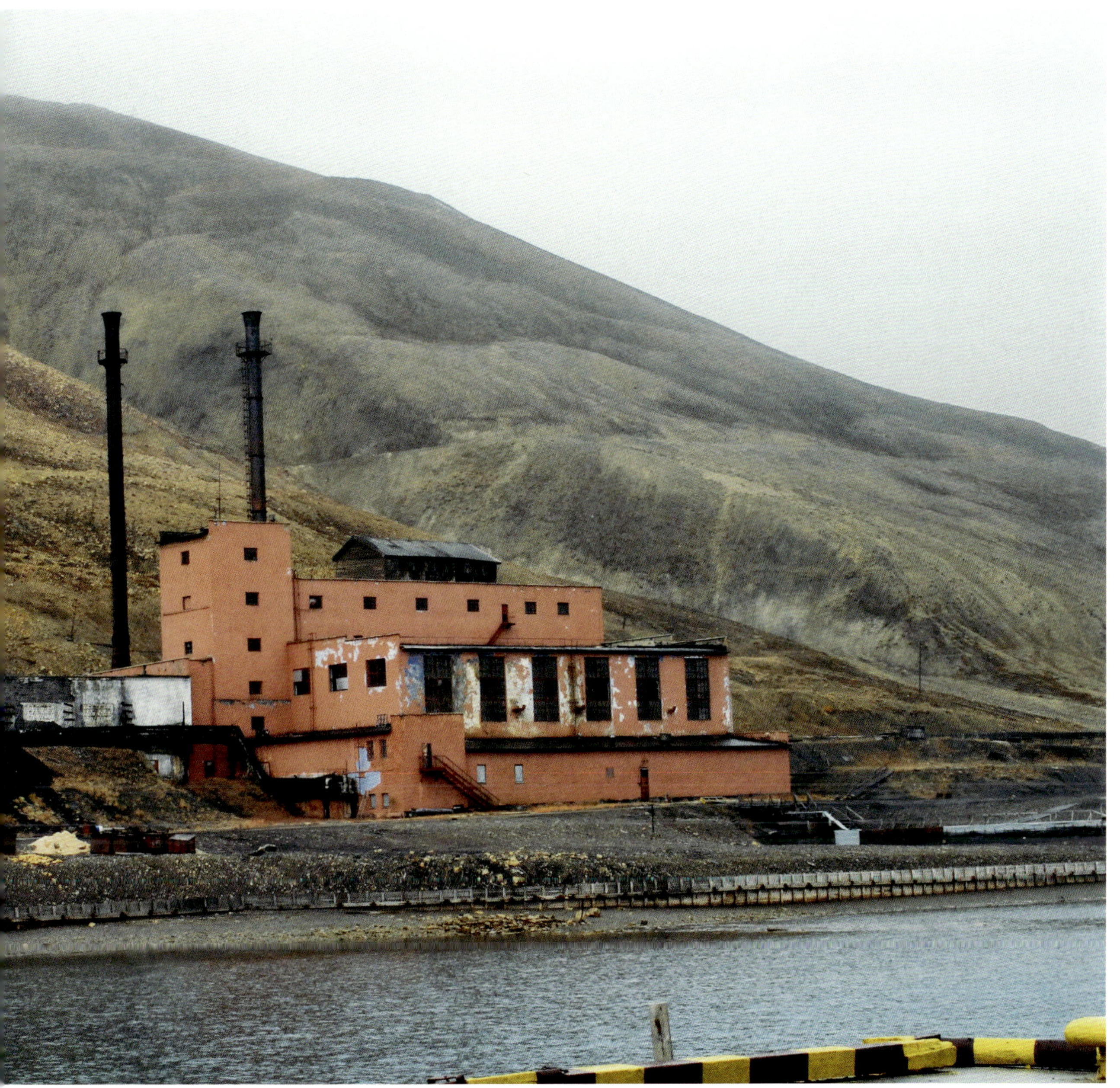

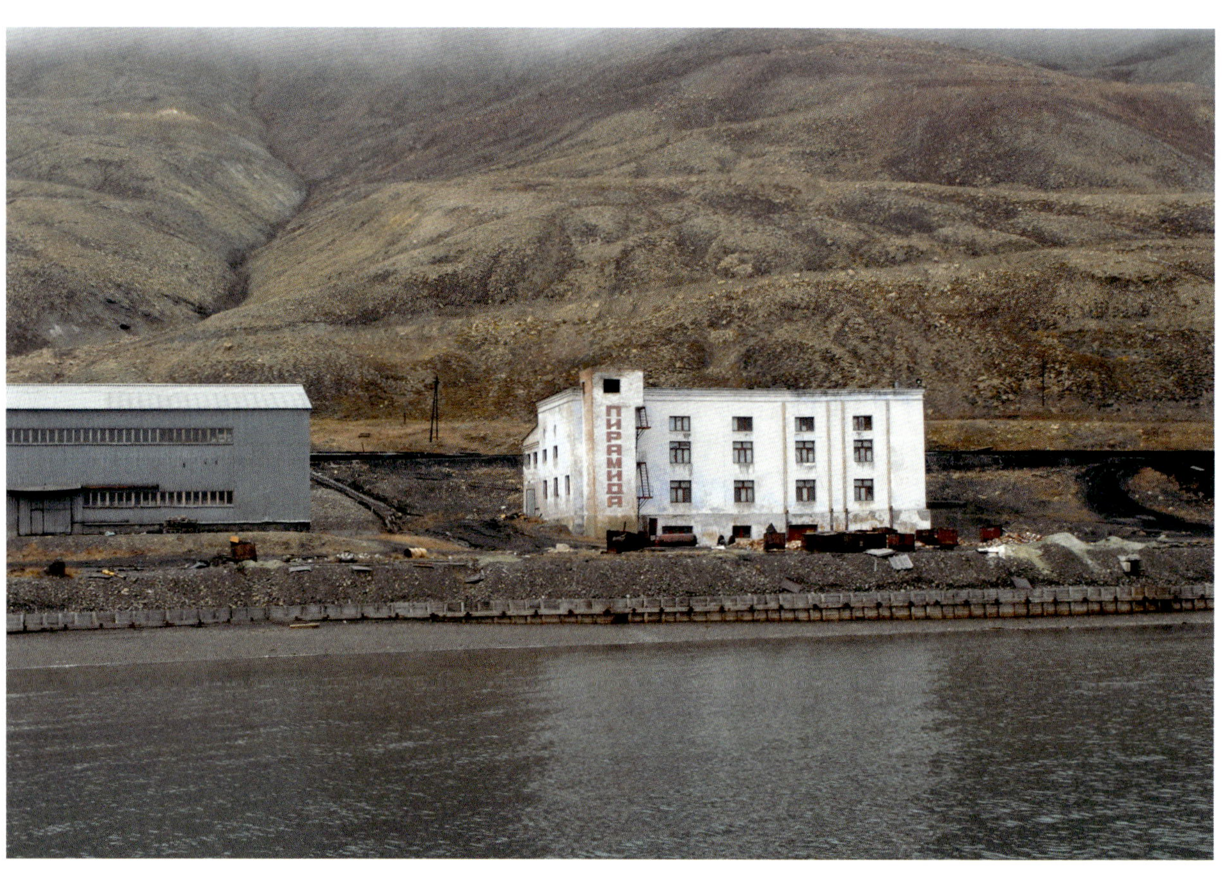
ПИРАМИДА

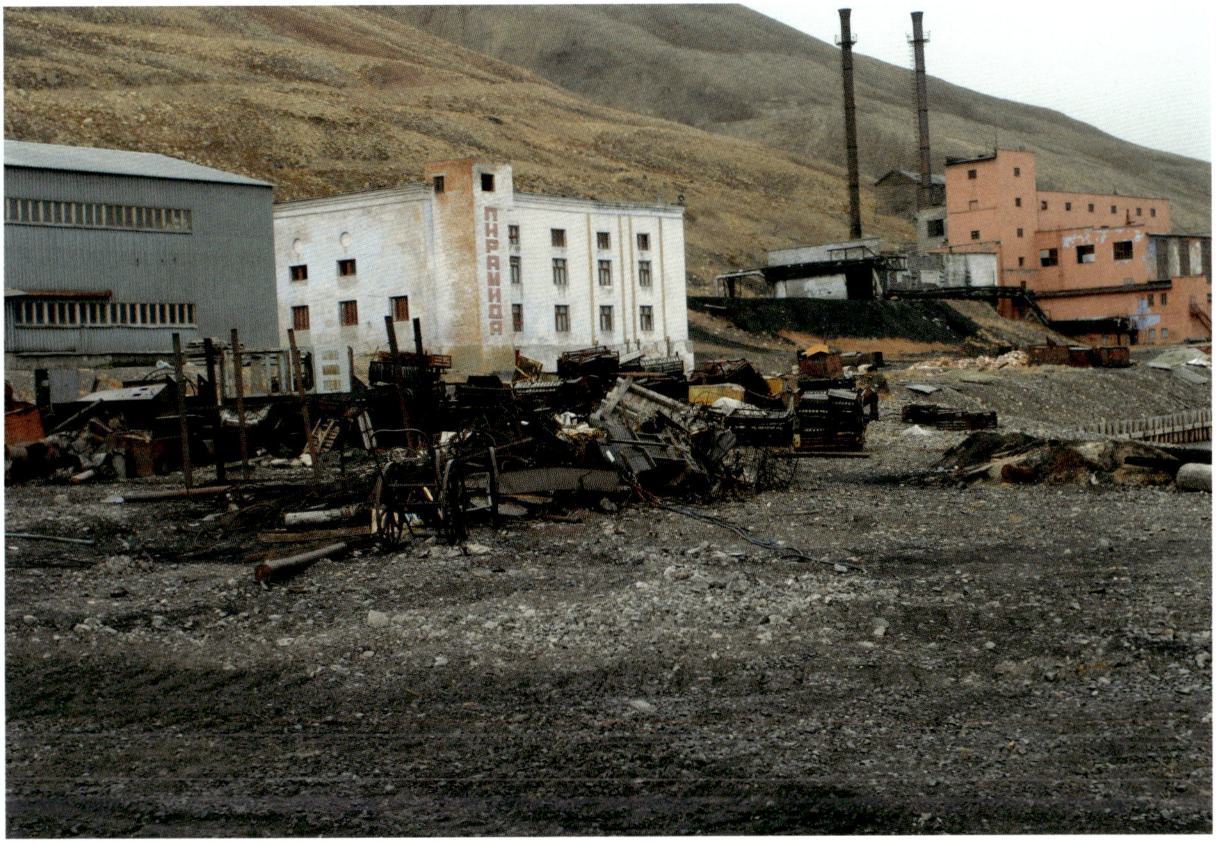

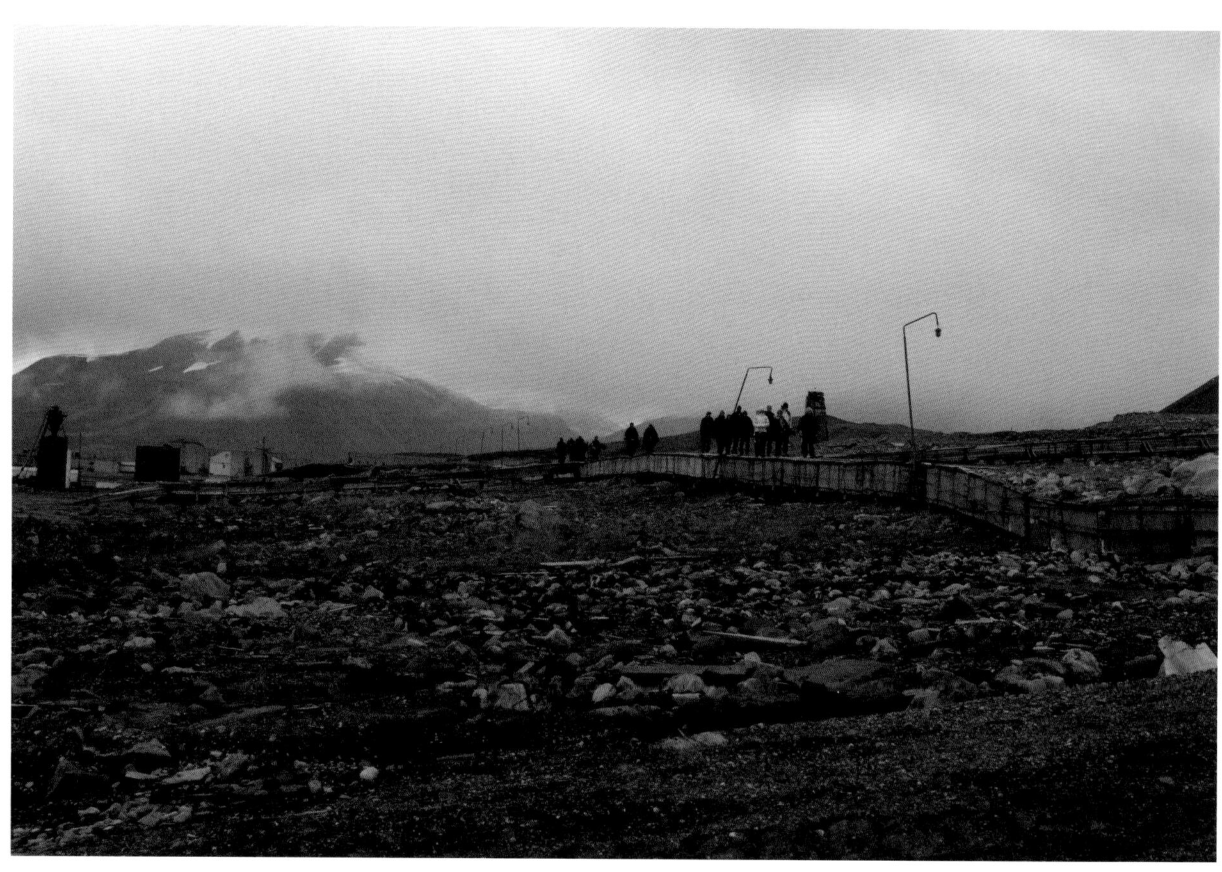

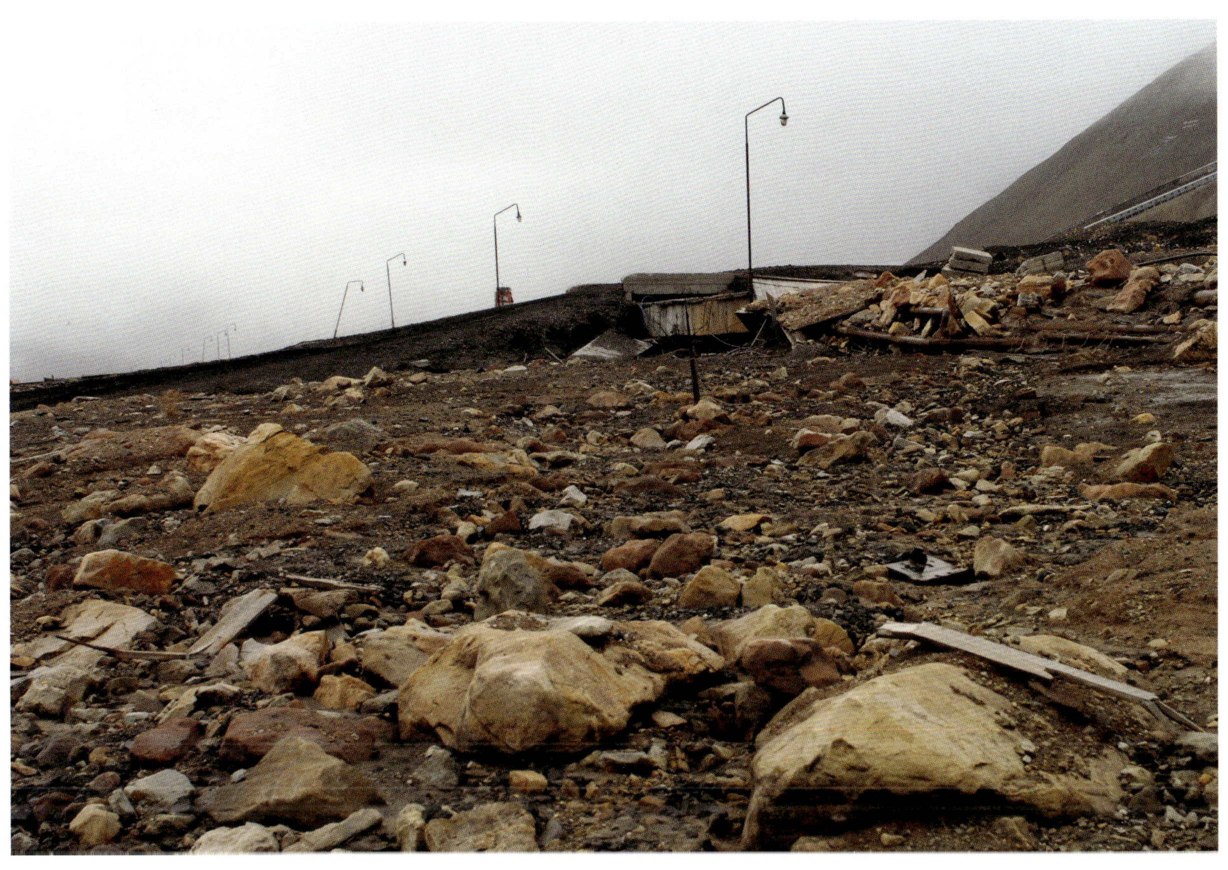

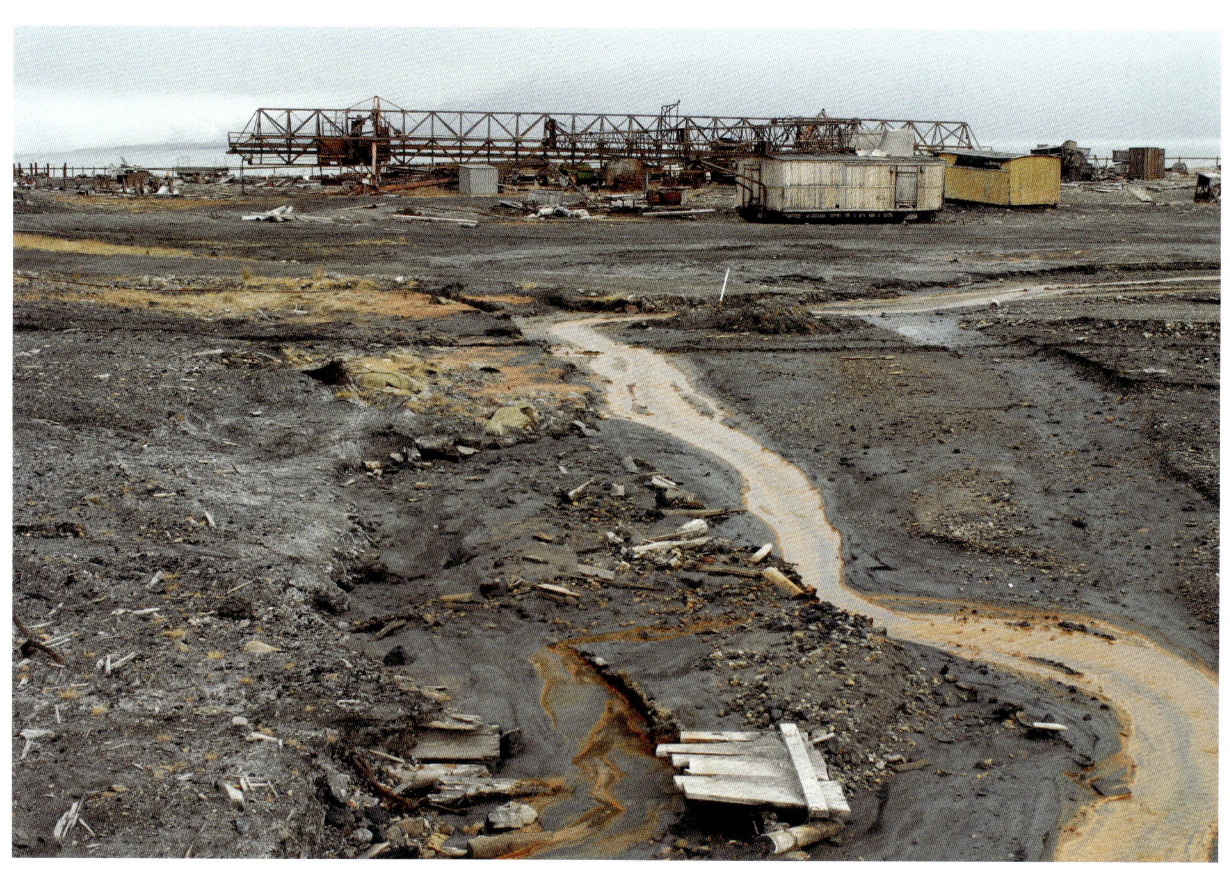

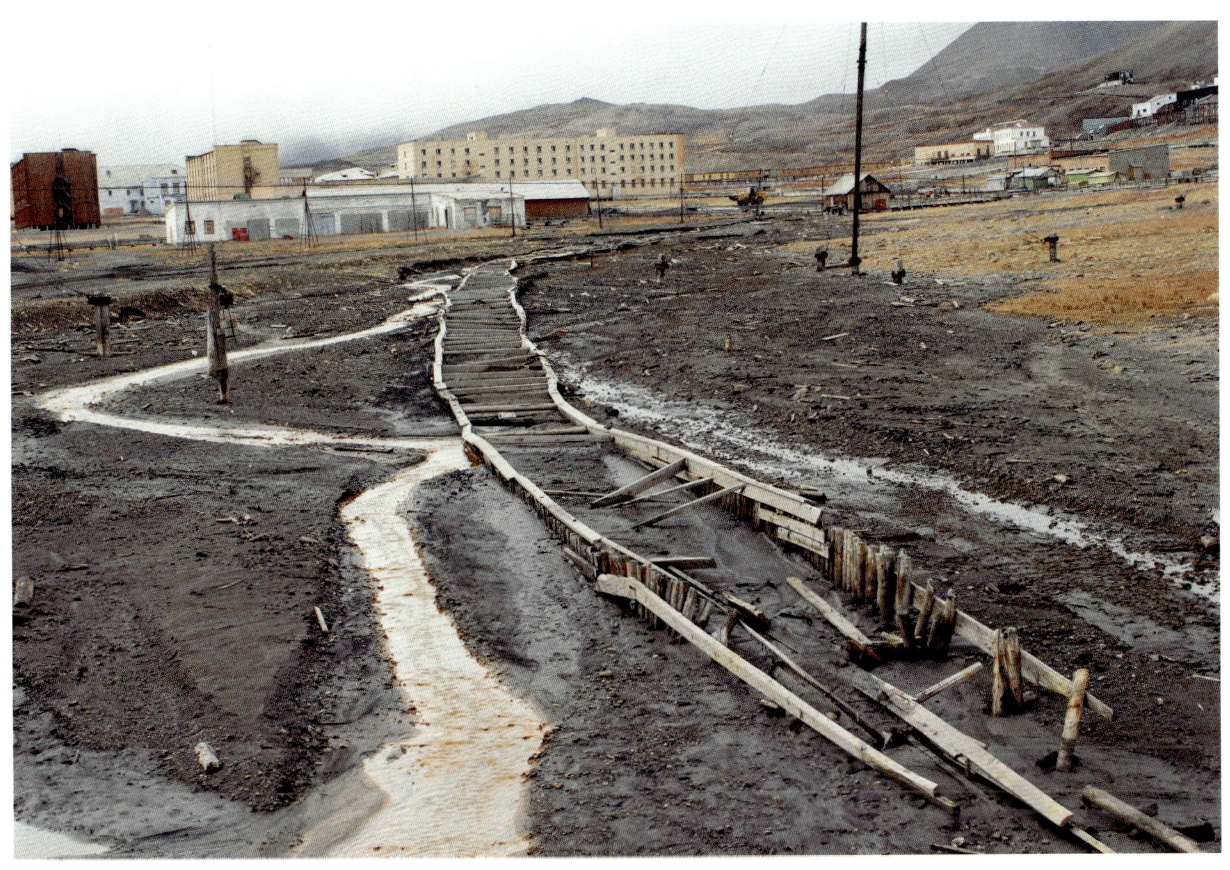

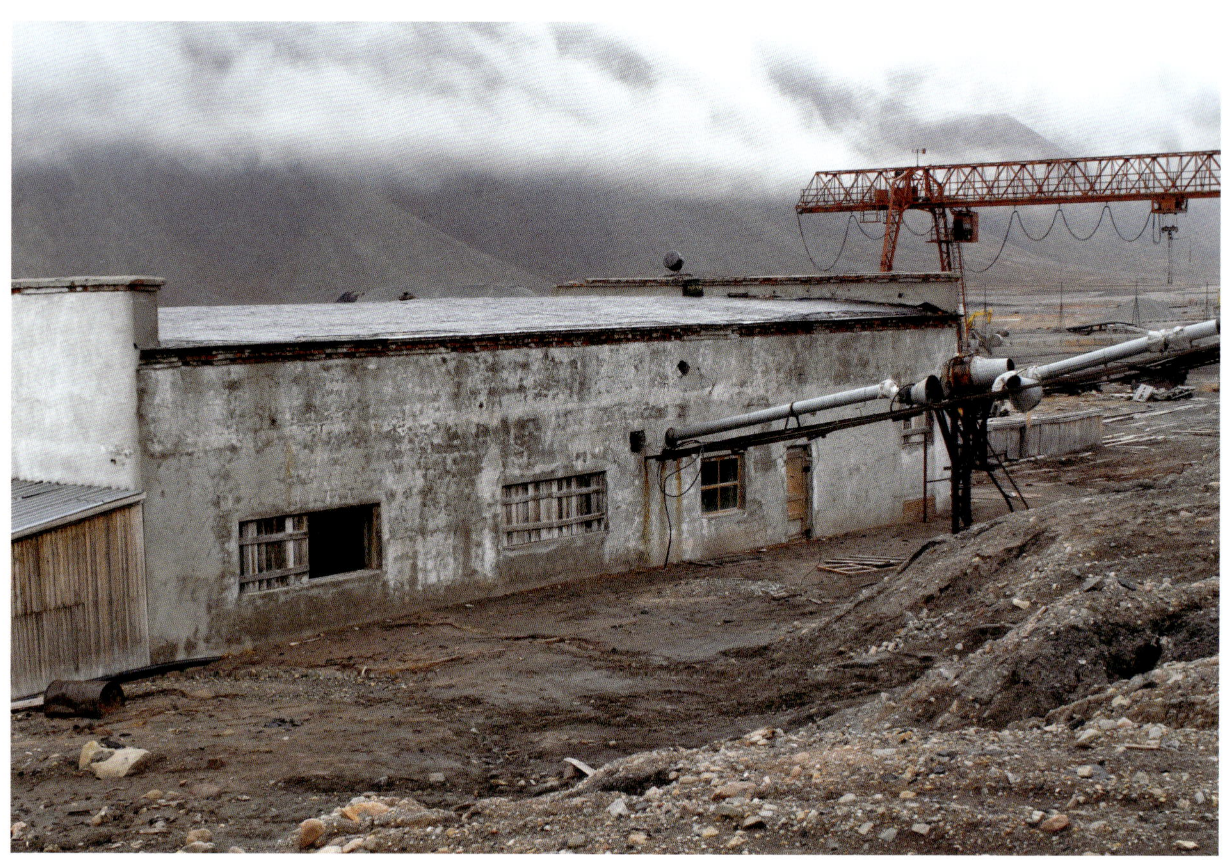

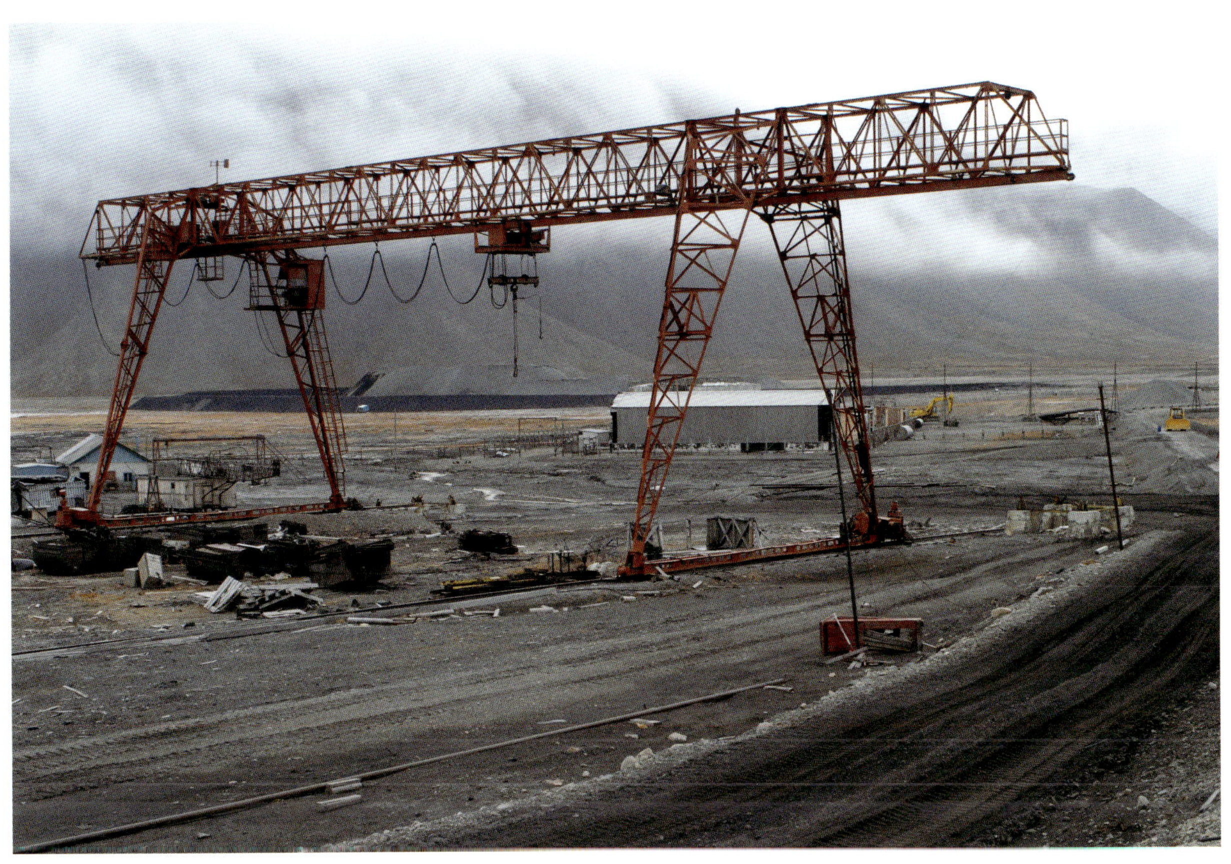

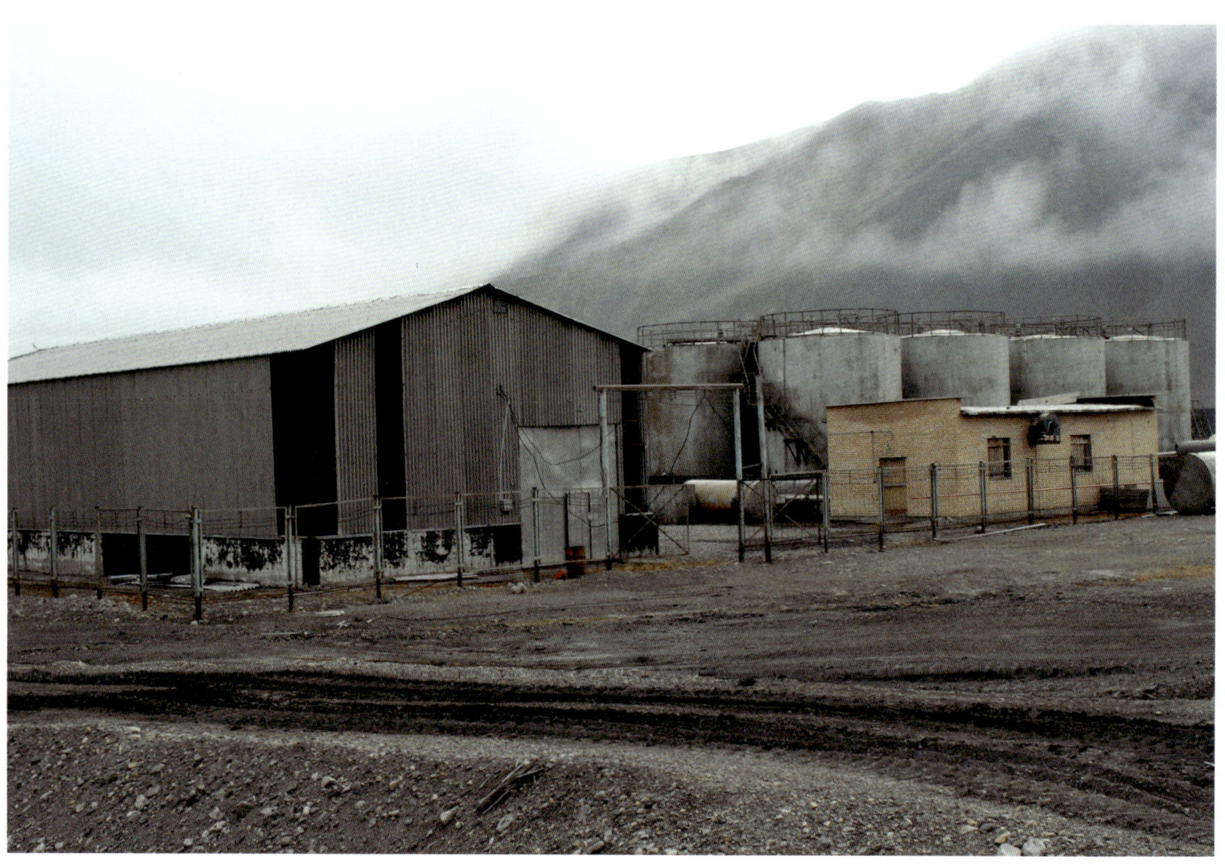

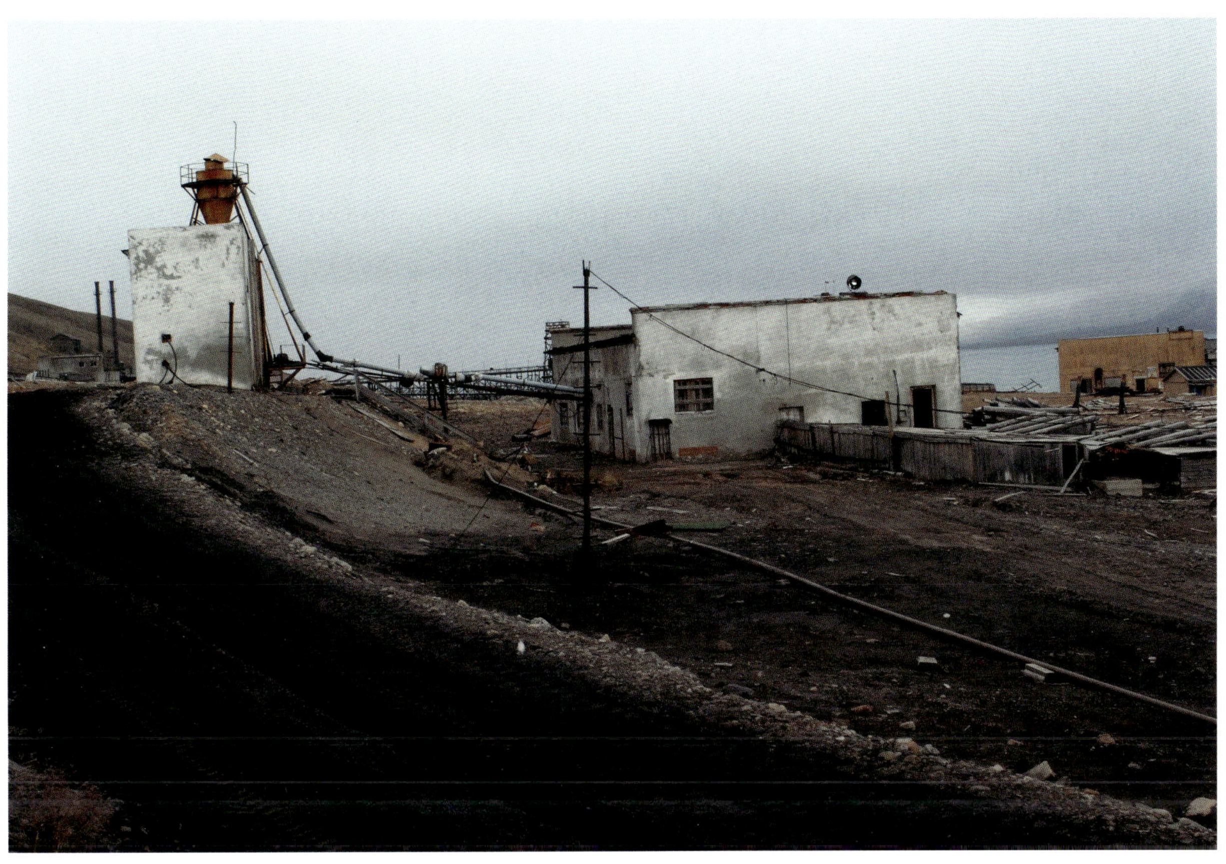

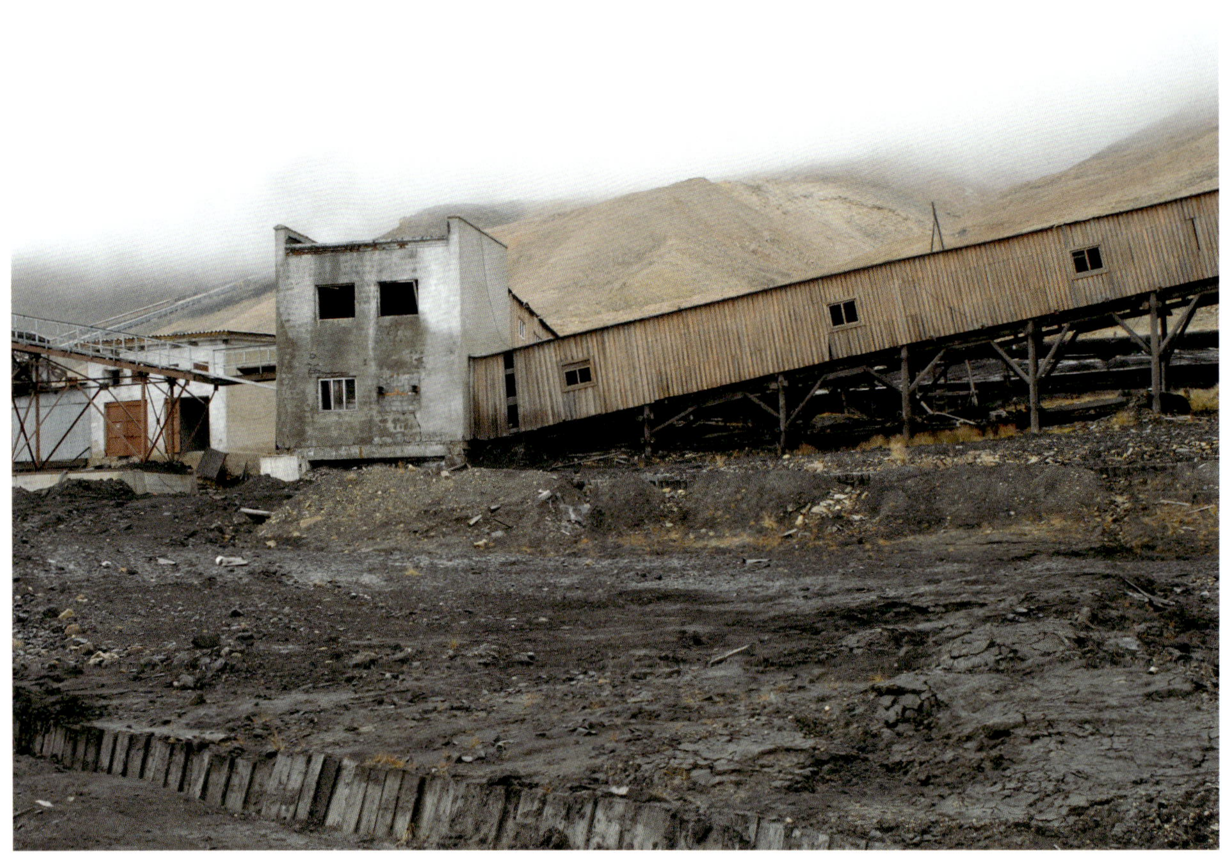

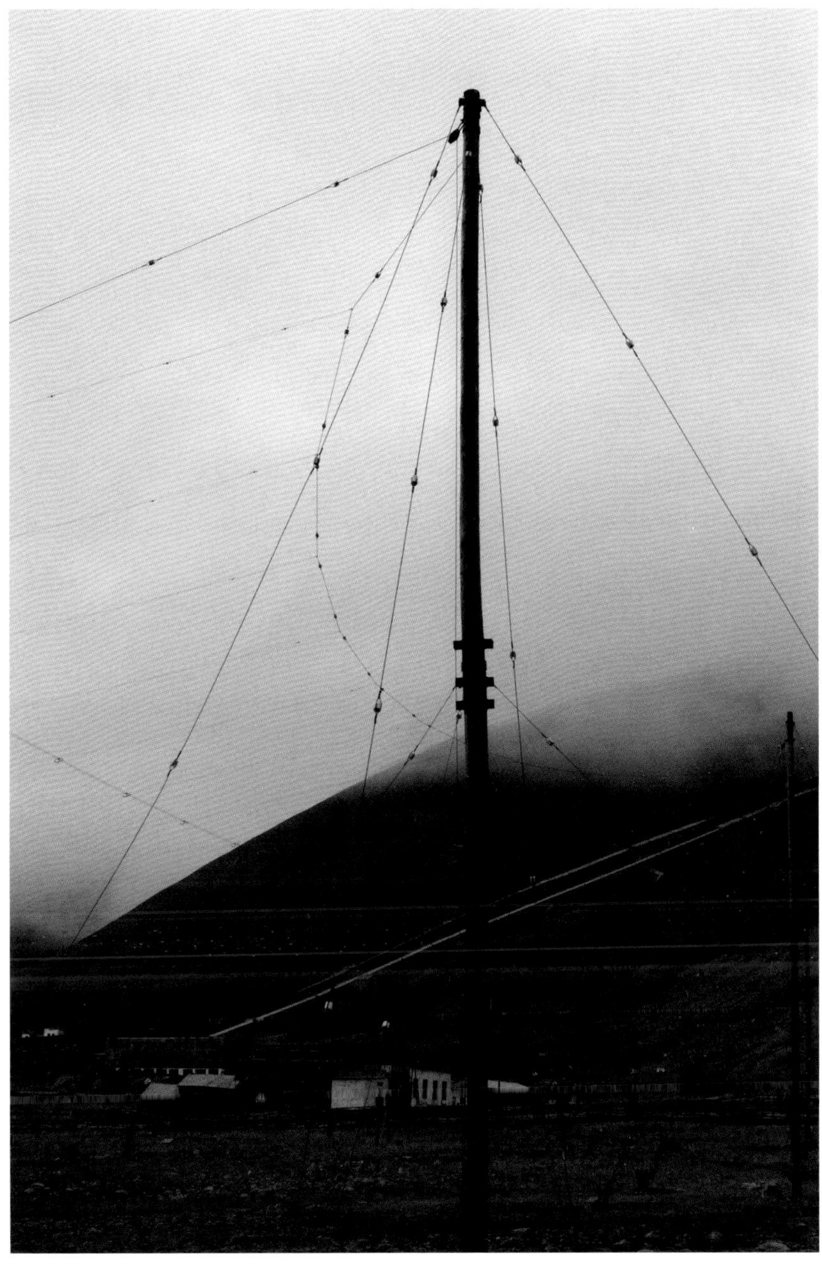

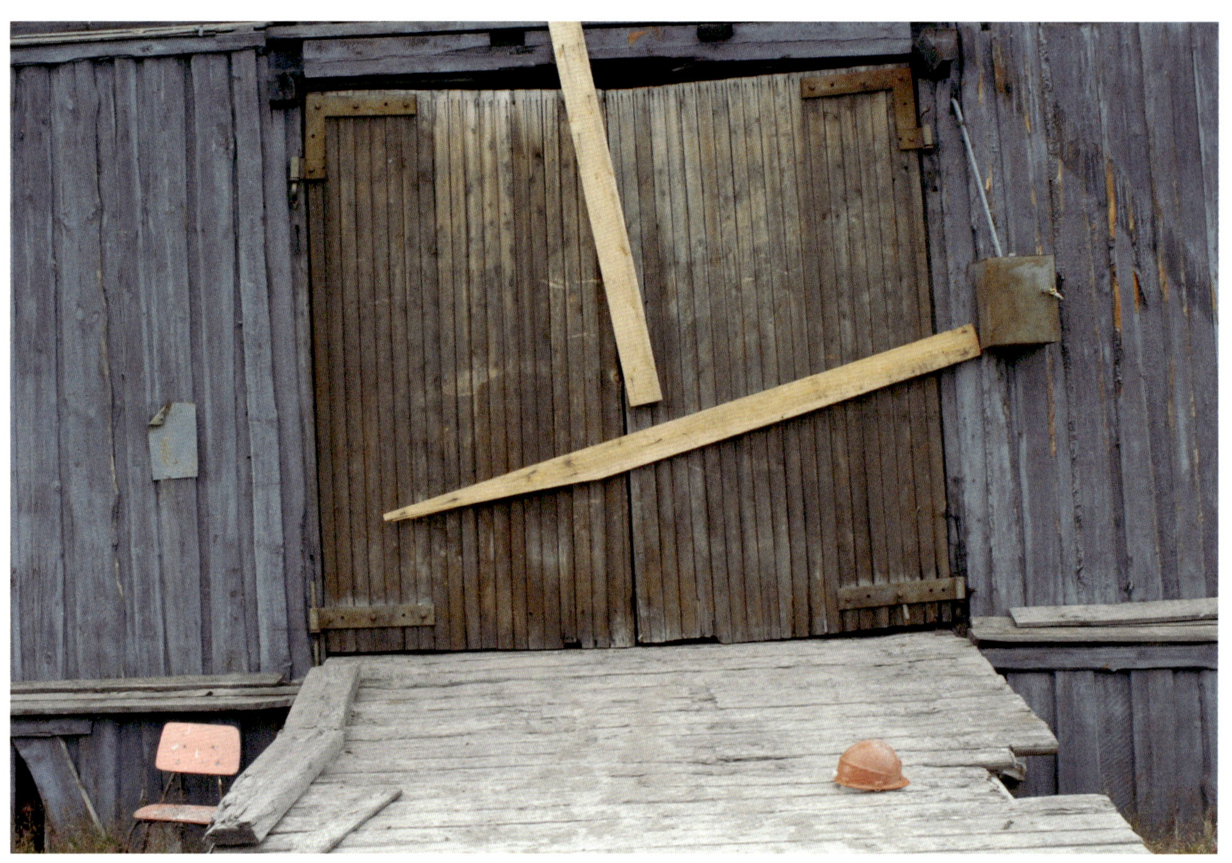

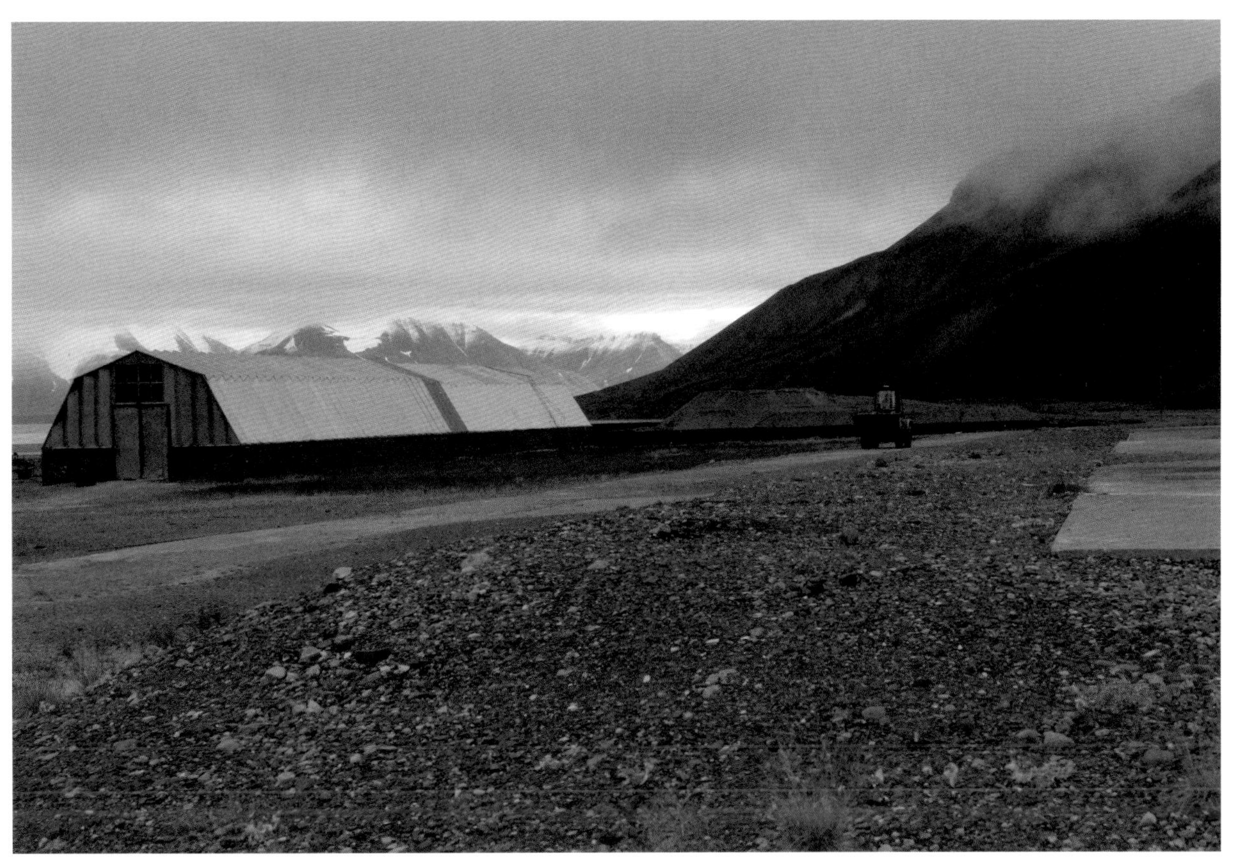

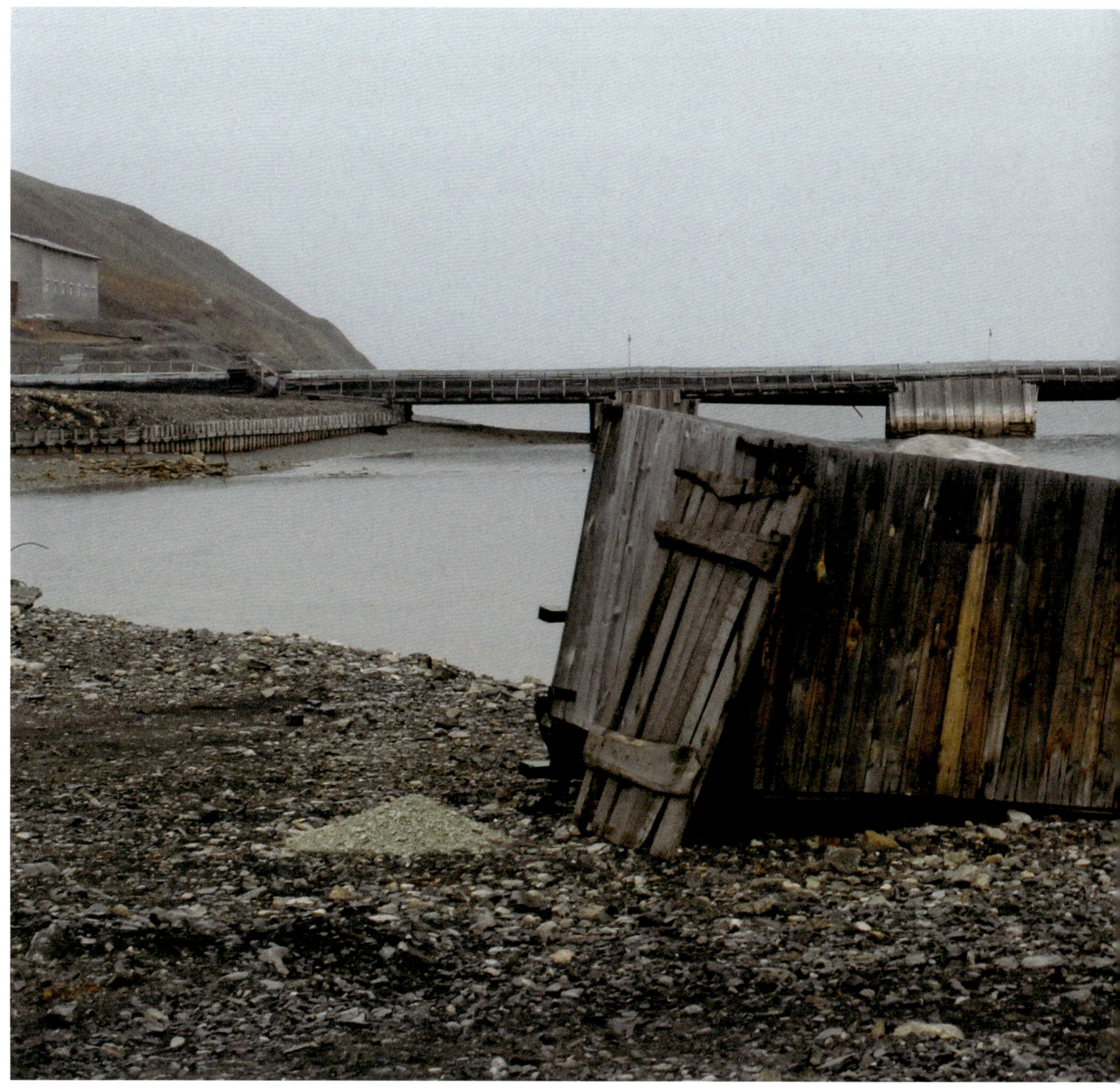

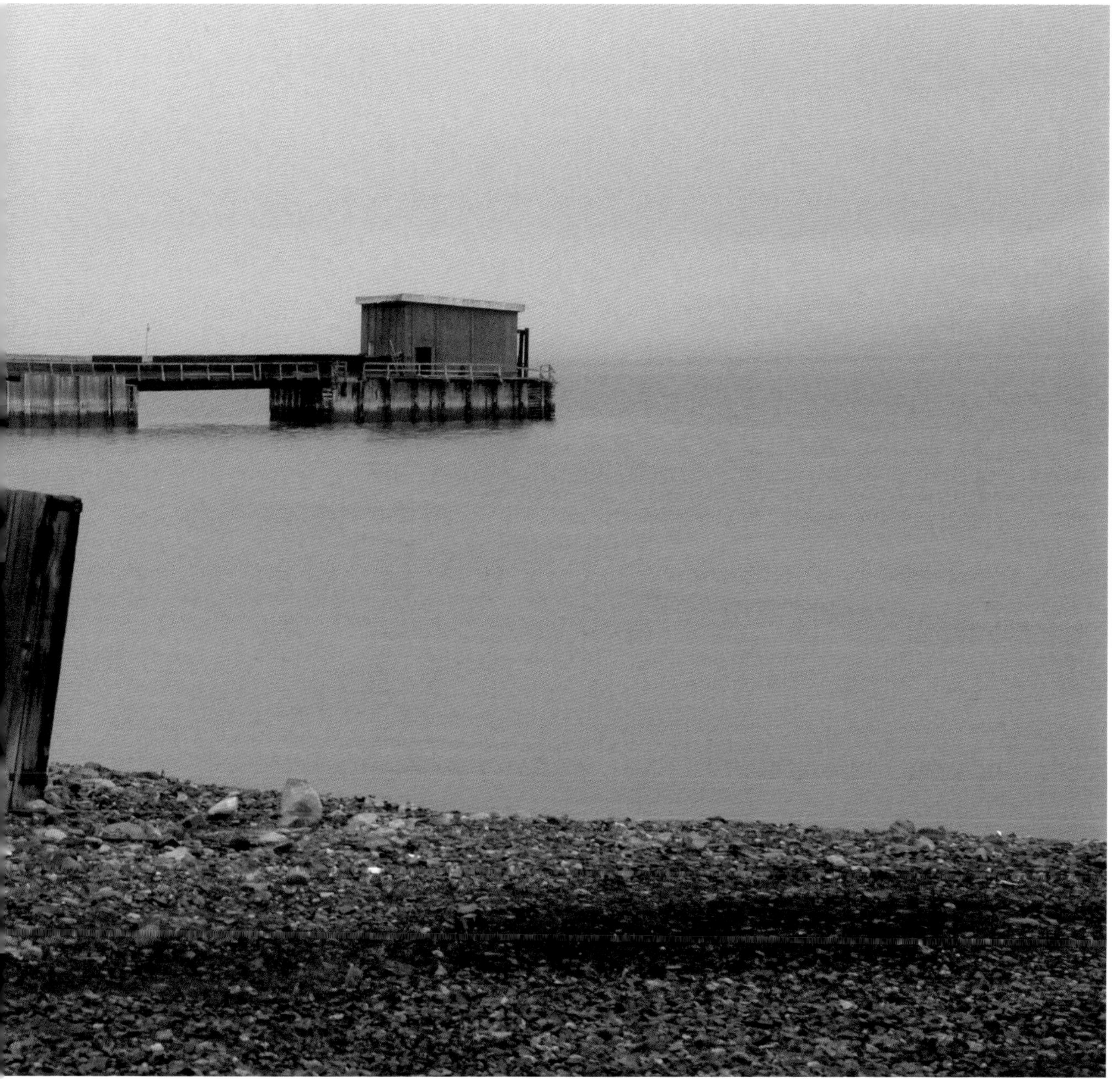

V
On the Way Back

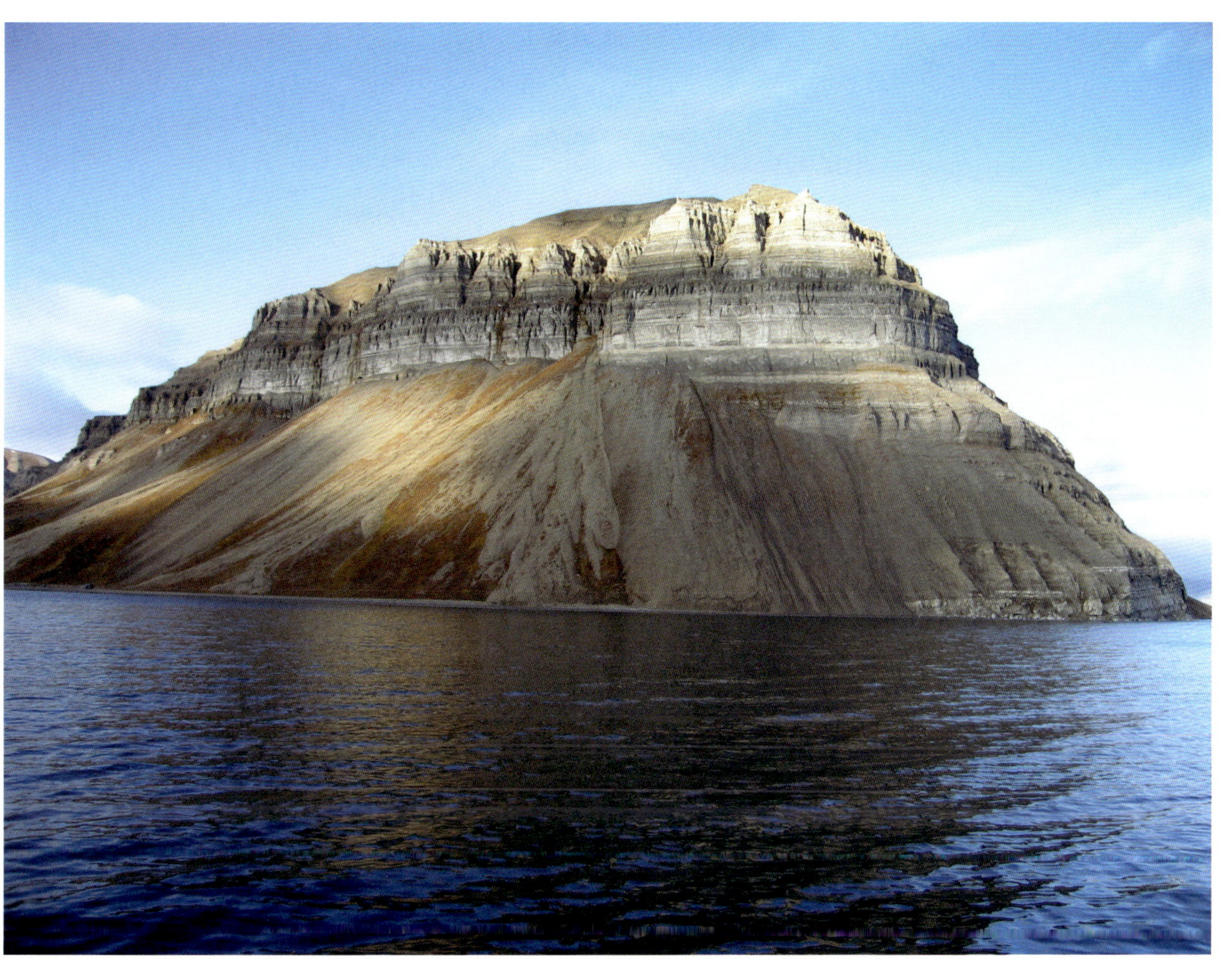

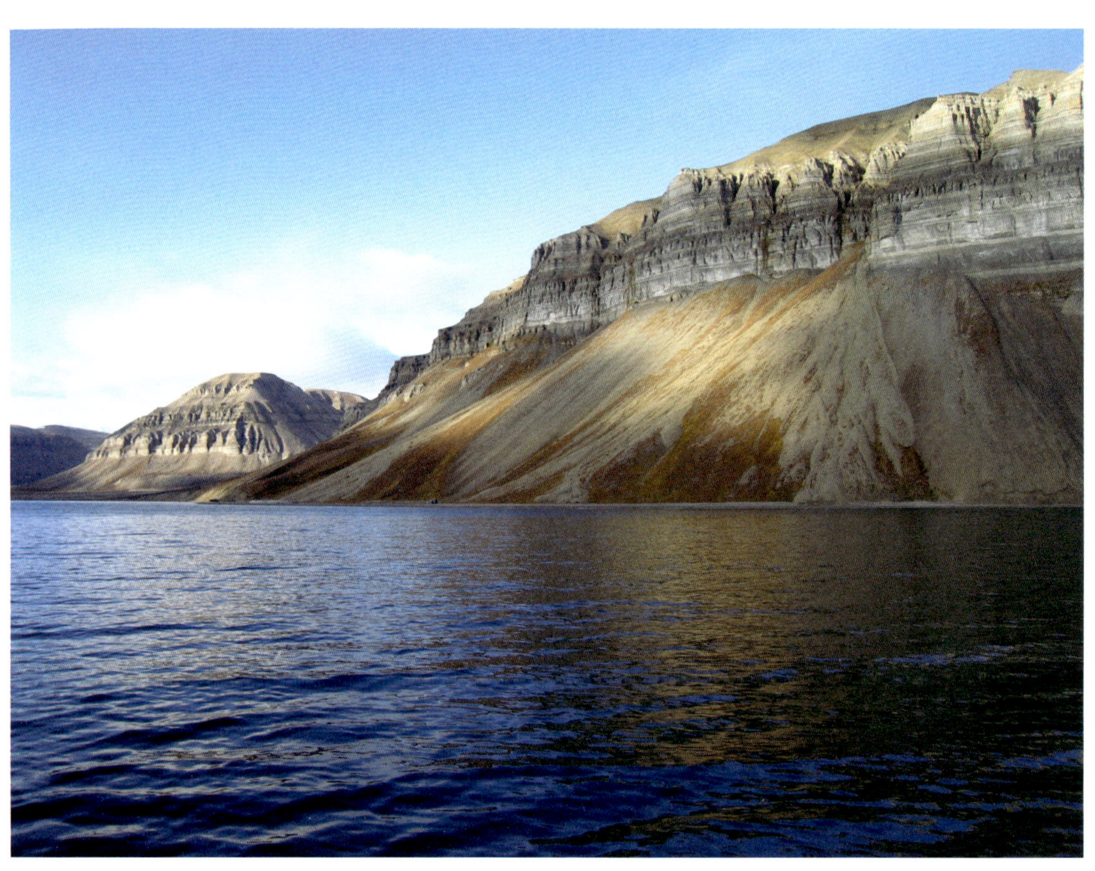

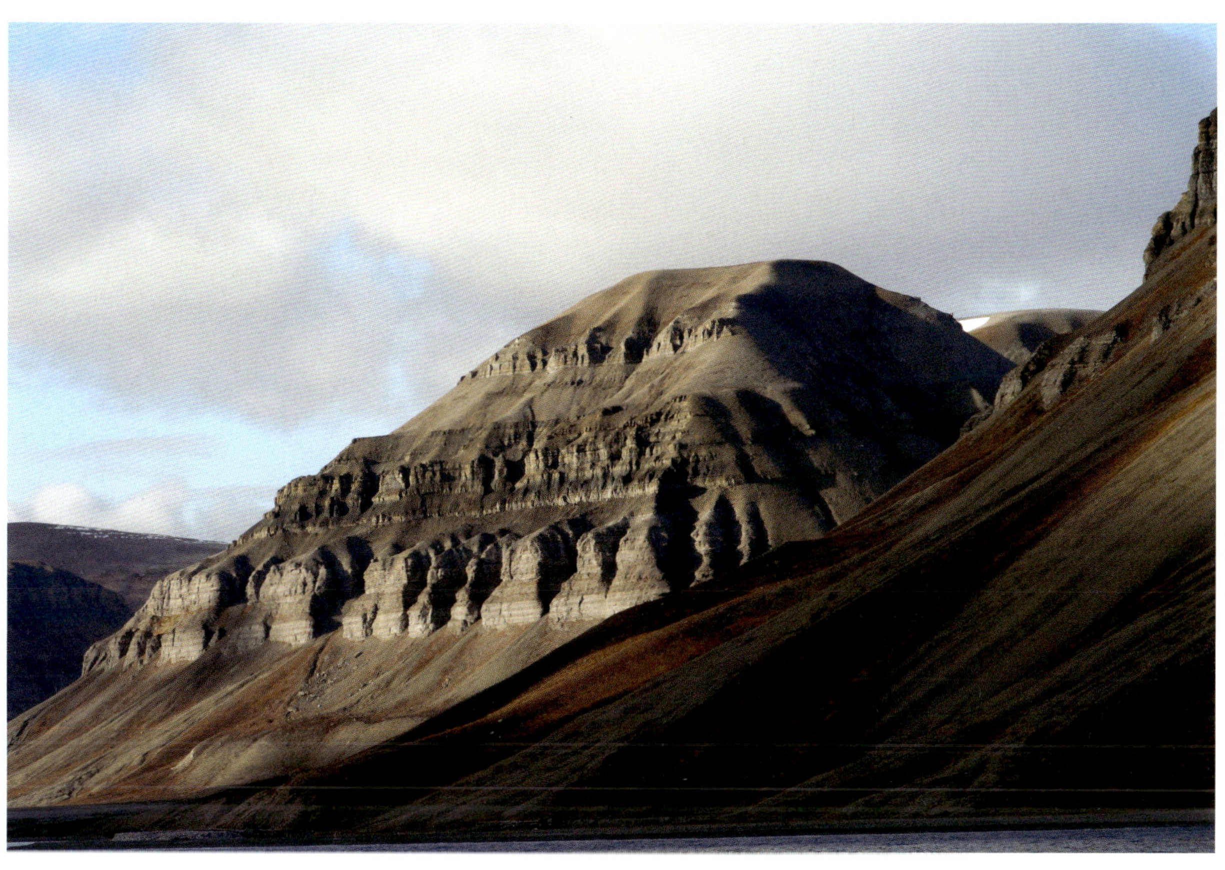

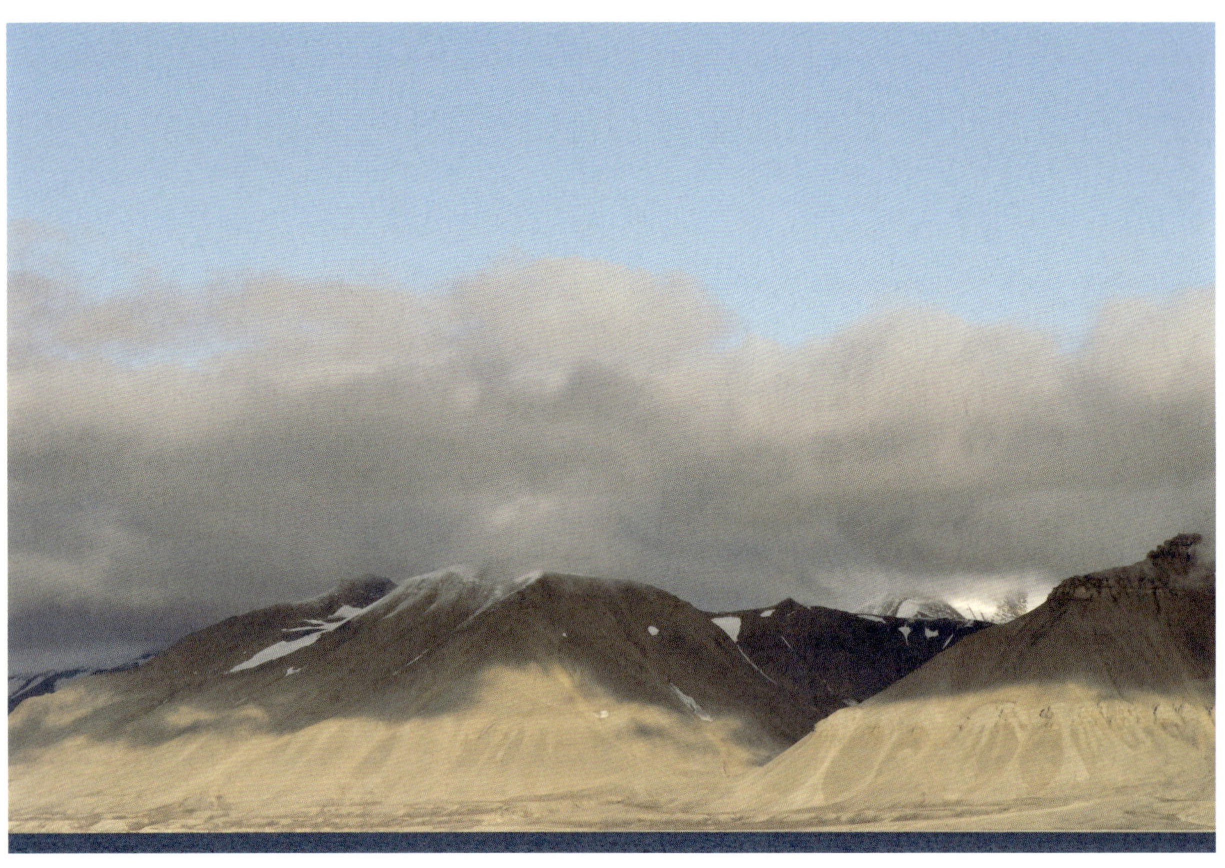

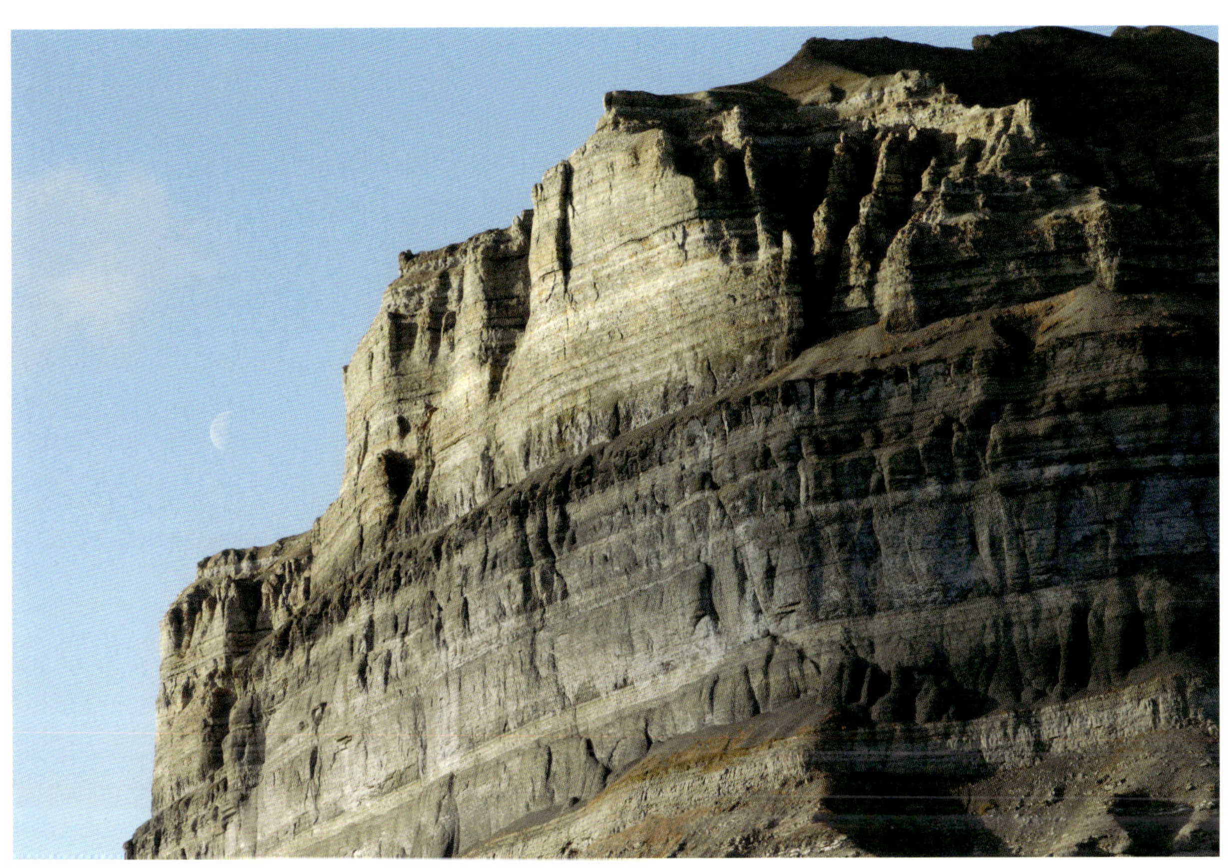

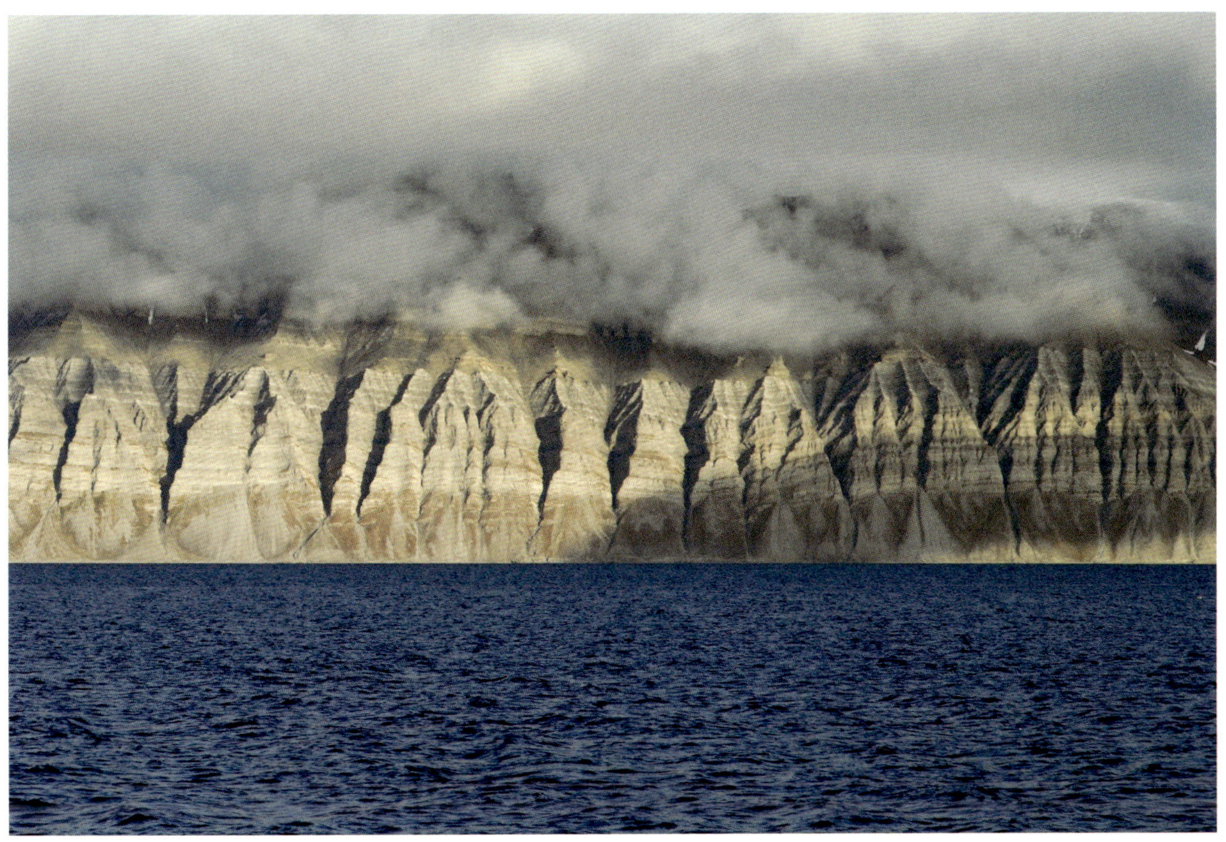

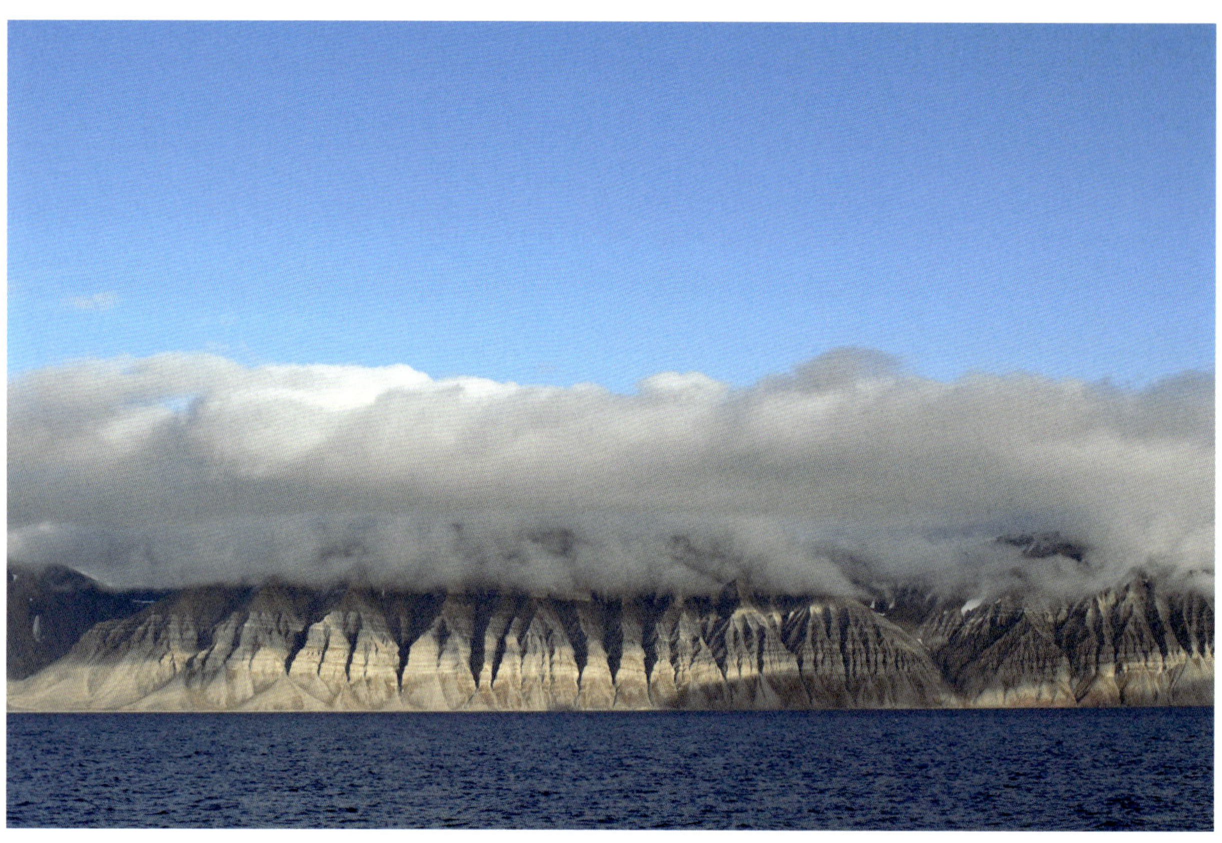

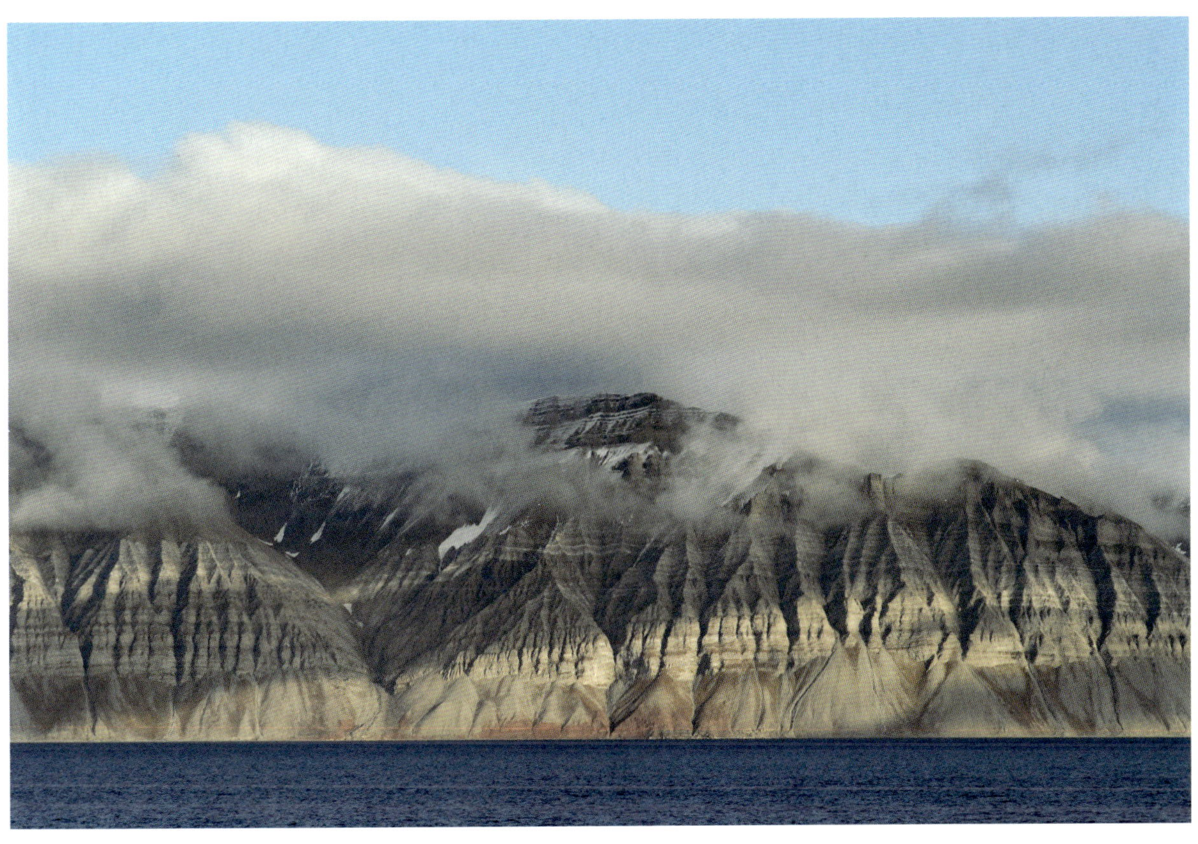

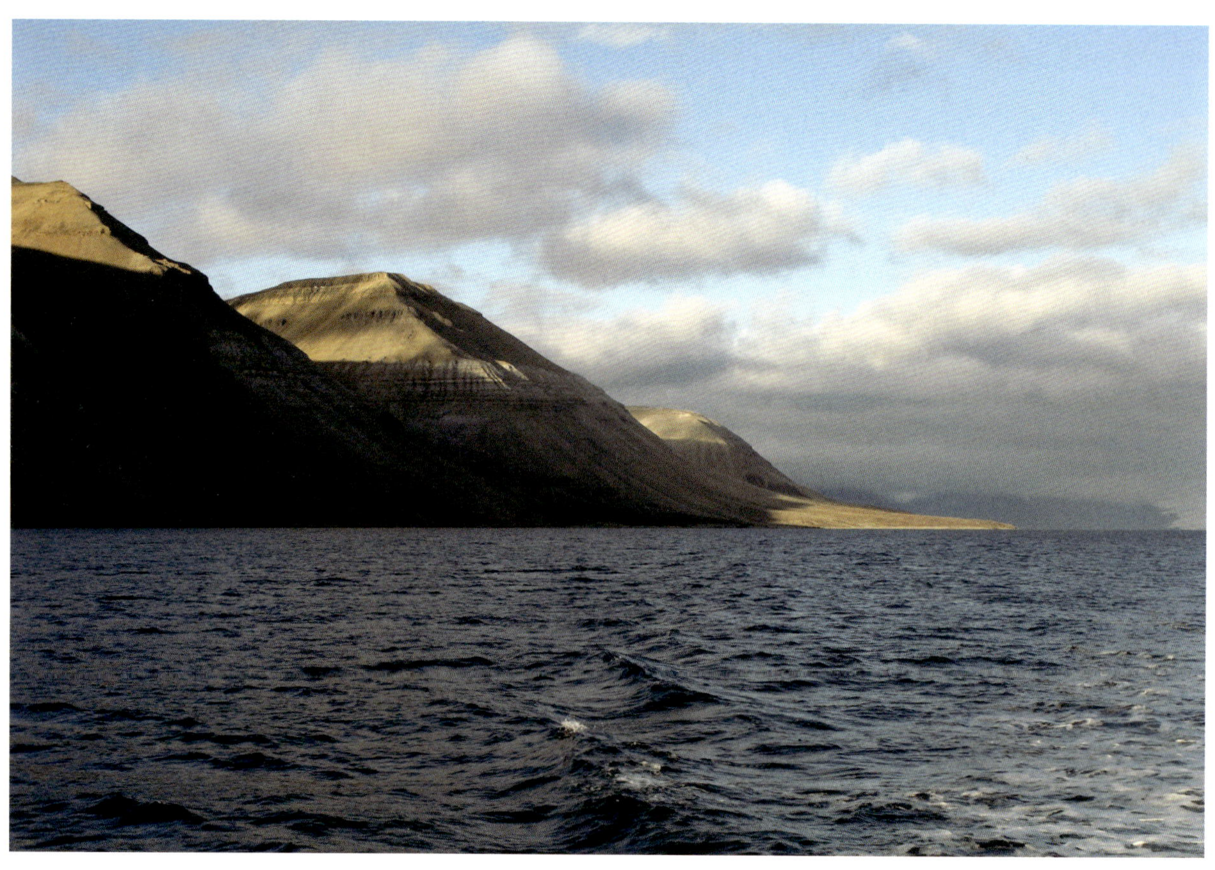

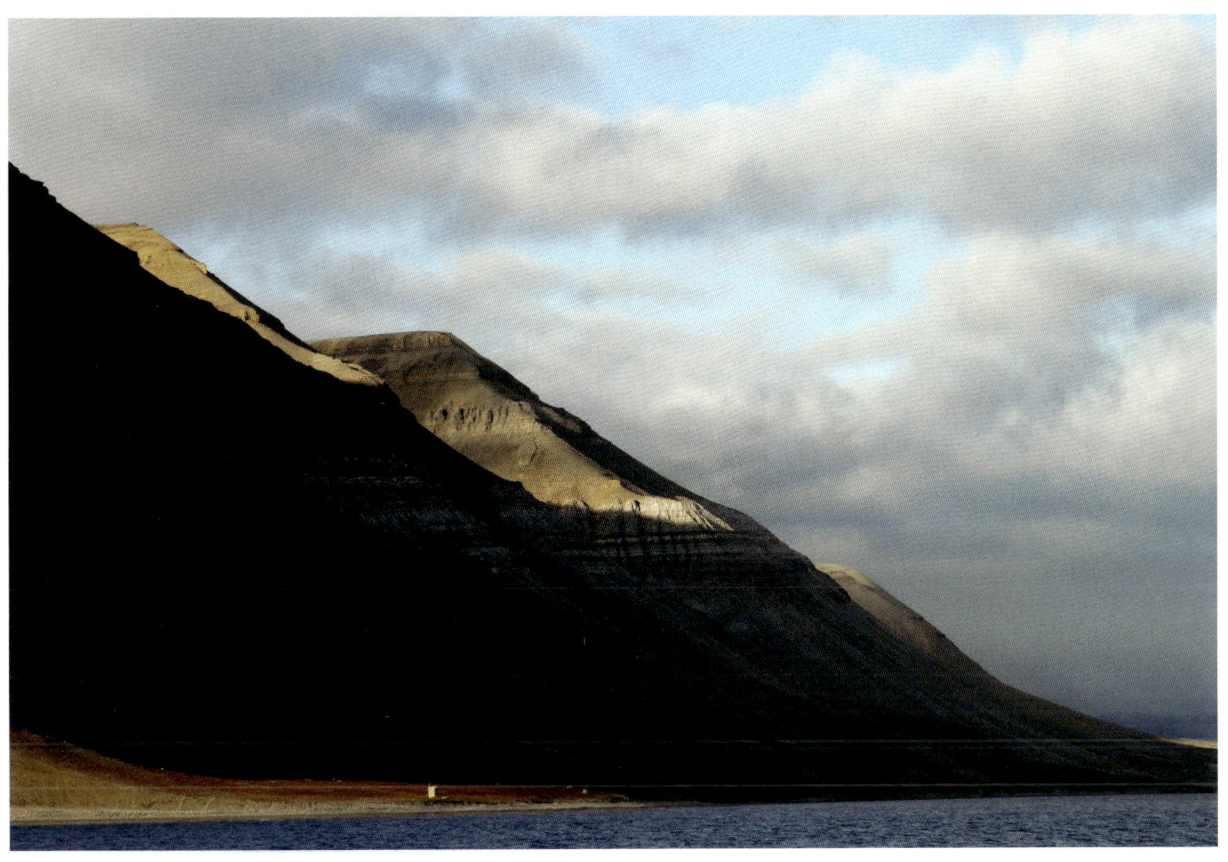

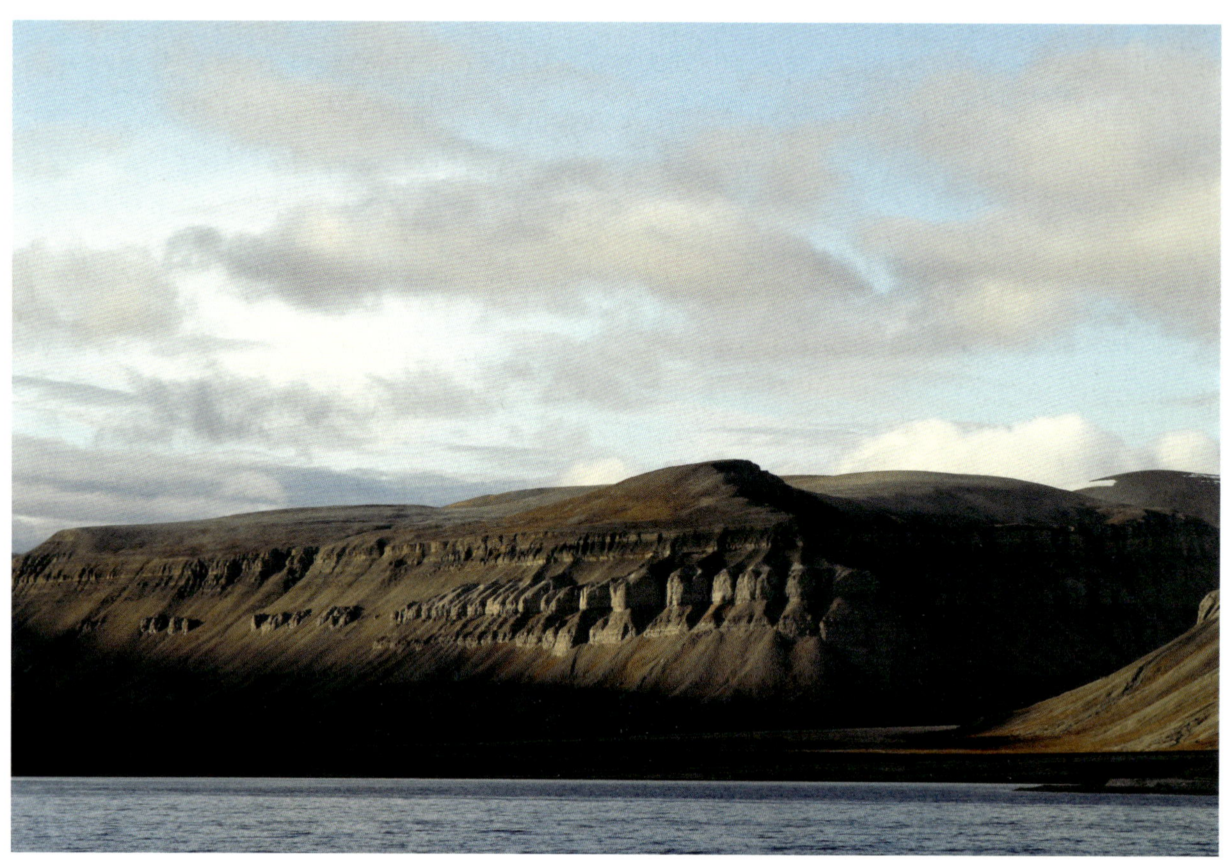

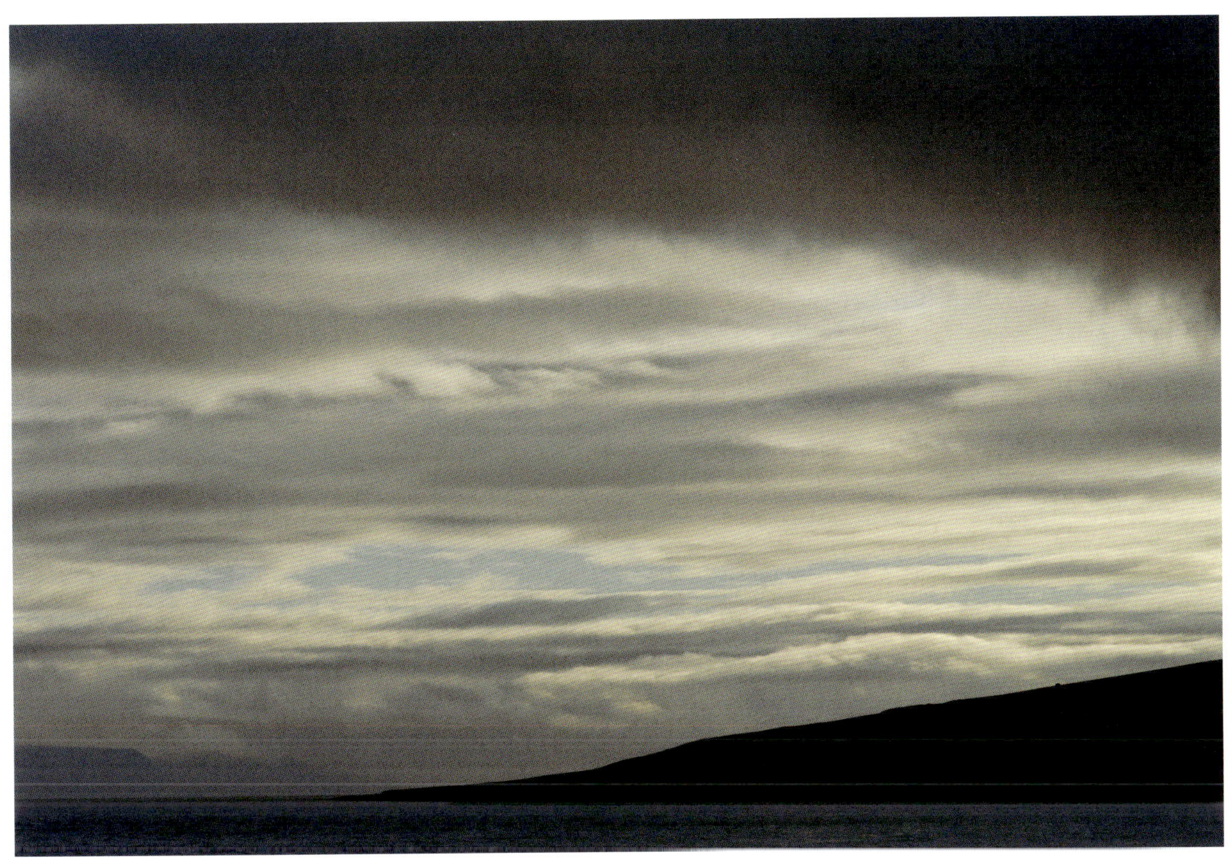

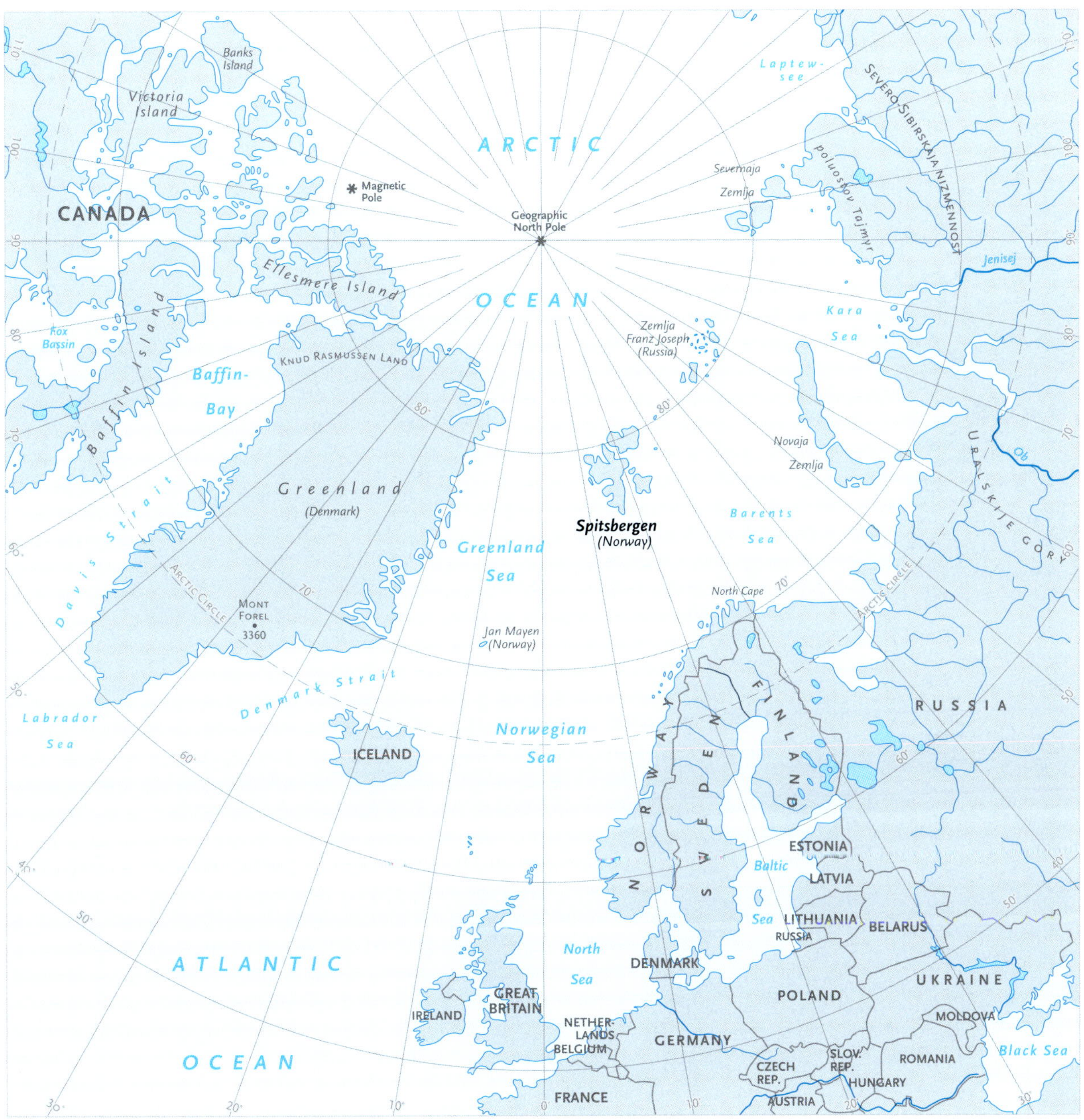

ARCTIC
OCEAN
Geographic North Pole
Magnetic Pole
CANADA
Banks Island
Victoria Island
Ellesmere Island
Baffin Island
Fox Bassin
Baffin-Bay
Knud Rasmussen Land
Greenland
(Denmark)
Davis Strait
Arctic Circle
Mont Forel
3360
Labrador Sea
Denmark Strait
Greenland Sea
Jan Mayen (Norway)
Spitsbergen
(Norway)
Zemlja Franz Joseph (Russia)
Severnaja Zemlja
Laptew-see
Severo-Sibirskaja Nizmennost
poluostrov Tajmyr
Jenisej
Kara Sea
Novaja Zemlja
Barents Sea
Uralskije Gory
Ob
North Cape
Norwegian Sea
ICELAND
NORWAY
SWEDEN
FINLAND
RUSSIA
ESTONIA
LATVIA
LITHUANIA
RUSSIA
BELARUS
Baltic Sea
North Sea
DENMARK
ATLANTIC
OCEAN
IRELAND
GREAT BRITAIN
NETHERLANDS
BELGIUM
GERMANY
POLAND
UKRAINE
MOLDOVA
CZECH REP.
SLOV. REP.
AUSTRIA
HUNGARY
ROMANIA
Black Sea
FRANCE

Separations: Bayermedia, München
Printing and binding: Passavia Druckservice

ISBN 978-3-8296-0393-5

A Schirmer/Mosel Production
www.schirmer-mosel.com